# THE COMPLETE
# RUNNER'S
## DAY-BY-DAY LOG
## 2015 CALENDAR

**Andrews McMeel**
**Publishing, LLC**
Kansas City · Sydney · London

## MARTY JEROME

# 2014

## January
| S | M | T | W | T | F | S |
|---|---|---|---|---|---|---|
|   |   |   | 1 | 2 | 3 | 4 |
| 5 | 6 | 7 | 8 | 9 | 10 | 11 |
| 12 | 13 | 14 | 15 | 16 | 17 | 18 |
| 19 | 20 | 21 | 22 | 23 | 24 | 25 |
| 26 | 27 | 28 | 29 | 30 | 31 |   |

## February
| S | M | T | W | T | F | S |
|---|---|---|---|---|---|---|
|   |   |   |   |   |   | 1 |
| 2 | 3 | 4 | 5 | 6 | 7 | 8 |
| 9 | 10 | 11 | 12 | 13 | 14 | 15 |
| 16 | 17 | 18 | 19 | 20 | 21 | 22 |
| 23 | 24 | 25 | 26 | 27 | 28 |   |

## March
| S | M | T | W | T | F | S |
|---|---|---|---|---|---|---|
|   |   |   |   |   |   | 1 |
| 2 | 3 | 4 | 5 | 6 | 7 | 8 |
| 9 | 10 | 11 | 12 | 13 | 14 | 15 |
| 16 | 17 | 18 | 19 | 20 | 21 | 22 |
| 23 | 24 | 25 | 26 | 27 | 28 | 29 |
| 30 | 31 |   |   |   |   |   |

## April
| S | M | T | W | T | F | S |
|---|---|---|---|---|---|---|
|   |   | 1 | 2 | 3 | 4 | 5 |
| 6 | 7 | 8 | 9 | 10 | 11 | 12 |
| 13 | 14 | 15 | 16 | 17 | 18 | 19 |
| 20 | 21 | 22 | 23 | 24 | 25 | 26 |
| 27 | 28 | 29 | 30 |   |   |   |

## May
| S | M | T | W | T | F | S |
|---|---|---|---|---|---|---|
|   |   |   |   | 1 | 2 | 3 |
| 4 | 5 | 6 | 7 | 8 | 9 | 10 |
| 11 | 12 | 13 | 14 | 15 | 16 | 17 |
| 18 | 19 | 20 | 21 | 22 | 23 | 24 |
| 25 | 26 | 27 | 28 | 29 | 30 | 31 |

## June
| S | M | T | W | T | F | S |
|---|---|---|---|---|---|---|
| 1 | 2 | 3 | 4 | 5 | 6 | 7 |
| 8 | 9 | 10 | 11 | 12 | 13 | 14 |
| 15 | 16 | 17 | 18 | 19 | 20 | 21 |
| 22 | 23 | 24 | 25 | 26 | 27 | 28 |
| 29 | 30 |   |   |   |   |   |

## July
| S | M | T | W | T | F | S |
|---|---|---|---|---|---|---|
|   |   | 1 | 2 | 3 | 4 | 5 |
| 6 | 7 | 8 | 9 | 10 | 11 | 12 |
| 13 | 14 | 15 | 16 | 17 | 18 | 19 |
| 20 | 21 | 22 | 23 | 24 | 25 | 26 |
| 27 | 28 | 29 | 30 | 31 |   |   |

## August
| S | M | T | W | T | F | S |
|---|---|---|---|---|---|---|
|   |   |   |   |   | 1 | 2 |
| 3 | 4 | 5 | 6 | 7 | 8 | 9 |
| 10 | 11 | 12 | 13 | 14 | 15 | 16 |
| 17 | 18 | 19 | 20 | 21 | 22 | 23 |
| 24 | 25 | 26 | 27 | 28 | 29 | 30 |
| 31 |   |   |   |   |   |   |

## September
| S | M | T | W | T | F | S |
|---|---|---|---|---|---|---|
|   | 1 | 2 | 3 | 4 | 5 | 6 |
| 7 | 8 | 9 | 10 | 11 | 12 | 13 |
| 14 | 15 | 16 | 17 | 18 | 19 | 20 |
| 21 | 22 | 23 | 24 | 25 | 26 | 27 |
| 28 | 29 | 30 |   |   |   |   |

## October
| S | M | T | W | T | F | S |
|---|---|---|---|---|---|---|
|   |   |   | 1 | 2 | 3 | 4 |
| 5 | 6 | 7 | 8 | 9 | 10 | 11 |
| 12 | 13 | 14 | 15 | 16 | 17 | 18 |
| 19 | 20 | 21 | 22 | 23 | 24 | 25 |
| 26 | 27 | 28 | 29 | 30 | 31 |   |

## November
| S | M | T | W | T | F | S |
|---|---|---|---|---|---|---|
|   |   |   |   |   |   | 1 |
| 2 | 3 | 4 | 5 | 6 | 7 | 8 |
| 9 | 10 | 11 | 12 | 13 | 14 | 15 |
| 16 | 17 | 18 | 19 | 20 | 21 | 22 |
| 23 | 24 | 25 | 26 | 27 | 28 | 29 |
| 30 |   |   |   |   |   |   |

## December
| S | M | T | W | T | F | S |
|---|---|---|---|---|---|---|
|   | 1 | 2 | 3 | 4 | 5 | 6 |
| 7 | 8 | 9 | 10 | 11 | 12 | 13 |
| 14 | 15 | 16 | 17 | 18 | 19 | 20 |
| 21 | 22 | 23 | 24 | 25 | 26 | 27 |
| 28 | 29 | 30 | 31 |   |   |   |

# 2016

## January
| S | M | T | W | T | F | S |
|---|---|---|---|---|---|---|
|   |   |   |   |   | 1 | 2 |
| 3 | 4 | 5 | 6 | 7 | 8 | 9 |
| 10 | 11 | 12 | 13 | 14 | 15 | 16 |
| 17 | 18 | 19 | 20 | 21 | 22 | 23 |
| 24 | 25 | 26 | 27 | 28 | 29 | 30 |
| 31 |   |   |   |   |   |   |

## February
| S | M | T | W | T | F | S |
|---|---|---|---|---|---|---|
|   | 1 | 2 | 3 | 4 | 5 | 6 |
| 7 | 8 | 9 | 10 | 11 | 12 | 13 |
| 14 | 15 | 16 | 17 | 18 | 19 | 20 |
| 21 | 22 | 23 | 24 | 25 | 26 | 27 |
| 28 | 29 |   |   |   |   |   |

## March
| S | M | T | W | T | F | S |
|---|---|---|---|---|---|---|
|   |   | 1 | 2 | 3 | 4 | 5 |
| 6 | 7 | 8 | 9 | 10 | 11 | 12 |
| 13 | 14 | 15 | 16 | 17 | 18 | 19 |
| 20 | 21 | 22 | 23 | 24 | 25 | 26 |
| 27 | 28 | 29 | 30 | 31 |   |   |

## April
| S | M | T | W | T | F | S |
|---|---|---|---|---|---|---|
|   |   |   |   |   | 1 | 2 |
| 3 | 4 | 5 | 6 | 7 | 8 | 9 |
| 10 | 11 | 12 | 13 | 14 | 15 | 16 |
| 17 | 18 | 19 | 20 | 21 | 22 | 23 |
| 24 | 25 | 26 | 27 | 28 | 29 | 30 |

## May
| S | M | T | W | T | F | S |
|---|---|---|---|---|---|---|
| 1 | 2 | 3 | 4 | 5 | 6 | 7 |
| 8 | 9 | 10 | 11 | 12 | 13 | 14 |
| 15 | 16 | 17 | 18 | 19 | 20 | 21 |
| 22 | 23 | 24 | 25 | 26 | 27 | 28 |
| 29 | 30 | 31 |   |   |   |   |

## June
| S | M | T | W | T | F | S |
|---|---|---|---|---|---|---|
|   |   |   | 1 | 2 | 3 | 4 |
| 5 | 6 | 7 | 8 | 9 | 10 | 11 |
| 12 | 13 | 14 | 15 | 16 | 17 | 18 |
| 19 | 20 | 21 | 22 | 23 | 24 | 25 |
| 26 | 27 | 28 | 29 | 30 |   |   |

## July
| S | M | T | W | T | F | S |
|---|---|---|---|---|---|---|
|   |   |   |   |   | 1 | 2 |
| 3 | 4 | 5 | 6 | 7 | 8 | 9 |
| 10 | 11 | 12 | 13 | 14 | 15 | 16 |
| 17 | 18 | 19 | 20 | 21 | 22 | 23 |
| 24 | 25 | 26 | 27 | 28 | 29 | 30 |
| 31 |   |   |   |   |   |   |

## August
| S | M | T | W | T | F | S |
|---|---|---|---|---|---|---|
|   | 1 | 2 | 3 | 4 | 5 | 6 |
| 7 | 8 | 9 | 10 | 11 | 12 | 13 |
| 14 | 15 | 16 | 17 | 18 | 19 | 20 |
| 21 | 22 | 23 | 24 | 25 | 26 | 27 |
| 28 | 29 | 30 | 31 |   |   |   |

## September
| S | M | T | W | T | F | S |
|---|---|---|---|---|---|---|
|   |   |   |   | 1 | 2 | 3 |
| 4 | 5 | 6 | 7 | 8 | 9 | 10 |
| 11 | 12 | 13 | 14 | 15 | 16 | 17 |
| 18 | 19 | 20 | 21 | 22 | 23 | 24 |
| 25 | 26 | 27 | 28 | 29 | 30 |   |

## October
| S | M | T | W | T | F | S |
|---|---|---|---|---|---|---|
|   |   |   |   |   |   | 1 |
| 2 | 3 | 4 | 5 | 6 | 7 | 8 |
| 9 | 10 | 11 | 12 | 13 | 14 | 15 |
| 16 | 17 | 18 | 19 | 20 | 21 | 22 |
| 23 | 24 | 25 | 26 | 27 | 28 | 29 |
| 30 | 31 |   |   |   |   |   |

## November
| S | M | T | W | T | F | S |
|---|---|---|---|---|---|---|
|   |   | 1 | 2 | 3 | 4 | 5 |
| 6 | 7 | 8 | 9 | 10 | 11 | 12 |
| 13 | 14 | 15 | 16 | 17 | 18 | 19 |
| 20 | 21 | 22 | 23 | 24 | 25 | 26 |
| 27 | 28 | 29 | 30 |   |   |   |

## December
| S | M | T | W | T | F | S |
|---|---|---|---|---|---|---|
|   |   |   |   | 1 | 2 | 3 |
| 4 | 5 | 6 | 7 | 8 | 9 | 10 |
| 11 | 12 | 13 | 14 | 15 | 16 | 17 |
| 18 | 19 | 20 | 21 | 22 | 23 | 24 |
| 25 | 26 | 27 | 28 | 29 | 30 | 31 |

# 2015

## January

| S | M | T | W | T | F | S |
|---|---|---|---|---|---|---|
|   |   |   |   | 1 | 2 | 3 |
| 4 | 5 | 6 | 7 | 8 | 9 | 10 |
| 11 | 12 | 13 | 14 | 15 | 16 | 17 |
| 18 | 19 | 20 | 21 | 22 | 23 | 24 |
| 25 | 26 | 27 | 28 | 29 | 30 | 31 |

## February

| S | M | T | W | T | F | S |
|---|---|---|---|---|---|---|
| 1 | 2 | 3 | 4 | 5 | 6 | 7 |
| 8 | 9 | 10 | 11 | 12 | 13 | 14 |
| 15 | 16 | 17 | 18 | 19 | 20 | 21 |
| 22 | 23 | 24 | 25 | 26 | 27 | 28 |

## March

| S | M | T | W | T | F | S |
|---|---|---|---|---|---|---|
| 1 | 2 | 3 | 4 | 5 | 6 | 7 |
| 8 | 9 | 10 | 11 | 12 | 13 | 14 |
| 15 | 16 | 17 | 18 | 19 | 20 | 21 |
| 22 | 23 | 24 | 25 | 26 | 27 | 28 |
| 29 | 30 | 31 |   |   |   |   |

## April

| S | M | T | W | T | F | S |
|---|---|---|---|---|---|---|
|   |   |   | 1 | 2 | 3 | 4 |
| 5 | 6 | 7 | 8 | 9 | 10 | 11 |
| 12 | 13 | 14 | 15 | 16 | 17 | 18 |
| 19 | 20 | 21 | 22 | 23 | 24 | 25 |
| 26 | 27 | 28 | 29 | 30 |   |   |

## May

| S | M | T | W | T | F | S |
|---|---|---|---|---|---|---|
|   |   |   |   |   | 1 | 2 |
| 3 | 4 | 5 | 6 | 7 | 8 | 9 |
| 10 | 11 | 12 | 13 | 14 | 15 | 16 |
| 17 | 18 | 19 | 20 | 21 | 22 | 23 |
| 24 | 25 | 26 | 27 | 28 | 29 | 30 |
| 31 |   |   |   |   |   |   |

## June

| S | M | T | W | T | F | S |
|---|---|---|---|---|---|---|
|   | 1 | 2 | 3 | 4 | 5 | 6 |
| 7 | 8 | 9 | 10 | 11 | 12 | 13 |
| 14 | 15 | 16 | 17 | 18 | 19 | 20 |
| 21 | 22 | 23 | 24 | 25 | 26 | 27 |
| 28 | 29 | 30 |   |   |   |   |

## July

| S | M | T | W | T | F | S |
|---|---|---|---|---|---|---|
|   |   |   | 1 | 2 | 3 | 4 |
| 5 | 6 | 7 | 8 | 9 | 10 | 11 |
| 12 | 13 | 14 | 15 | 16 | 17 | 18 |
| 19 | 20 | 21 | 22 | 23 | 24 | 25 |
| 26 | 27 | 28 | 29 | 30 | 31 |   |

## August

| S | M | T | W | T | F | S |
|---|---|---|---|---|---|---|
|   |   |   |   |   |   | 1 |
| 2 | 3 | 4 | 5 | 6 | 7 | 8 |
| 9 | 10 | 11 | 12 | 13 | 14 | 15 |
| 16 | 17 | 18 | 19 | 20 | 21 | 22 |
| 23 | 24 | 25 | 26 | 27 | 28 | 29 |
| 30 | 31 |   |   |   |   |   |

## September

| S | M | T | W | T | F | S |
|---|---|---|---|---|---|---|
|   |   | 1 | 2 | 3 | 4 | 5 |
| 6 | 7 | 8 | 9 | 10 | 11 | 12 |
| 13 | 14 | 15 | 16 | 17 | 18 | 19 |
| 20 | 21 | 22 | 23 | 24 | 25 | 26 |
| 27 | 28 | 29 | 30 |   |   |   |

## October

| S | M | T | W | T | F | S |
|---|---|---|---|---|---|---|
|   |   |   |   | 1 | 2 | 3 |
| 4 | 5 | 6 | 7 | 8 | 9 | 10 |
| 11 | 12 | 13 | 14 | 15 | 16 | 17 |
| 18 | 19 | 20 | 21 | 22 | 23 | 24 |
| 25 | 26 | 27 | 28 | 29 | 30 | 31 |

## November

| S | M | T | W | T | F | S |
|---|---|---|---|---|---|---|
| 1 | 2 | 3 | 4 | 5 | 6 | 7 |
| 8 | 9 | 10 | 11 | 12 | 13 | 14 |
| 15 | 16 | 17 | 18 | 19 | 20 | 21 |
| 22 | 23 | 24 | 25 | 26 | 27 | 28 |
| 29 | 30 |   |   |   |   |   |

## December

| S | M | T | W | T | F | S |
|---|---|---|---|---|---|---|
|   |   | 1 | 2 | 3 | 4 | 5 |
| 6 | 7 | 8 | 9 | 10 | 11 | 12 |
| 13 | 14 | 15 | 16 | 17 | 18 | 19 |
| 20 | 21 | 22 | 23 | 24 | 25 | 26 |
| 27 | 28 | 29 | 30 | 31 |   |   |

# INTRODUCTION

Running teems with comeback stories. Our hearts swell at the successful athlete struck down by disease, injury, or high misfortune but who miraculously returns to meet or exceed past glories. These tales stoke headlines, tweets, and blogs. Less attention is flashed on the ordinary person leading an unremarkable life (if such a thing is possible), who stumbles into running as if into divine intervention. A life is reborn, and with it, new purpose, relationships, values, and ways of negotiating daily living. These stories happen all around us, though we rarely hear them, unless circumstances grab media attention. Many runners don't know how to talk about them; some haven't even recognized the elemental changes they've undergone. Yet these stories are worth seeking. If there's any single quality the owners of these stories share, it's an abiding sense of humility.

It can occur at any time in life. Finishing a marathon in 3,851st place at a little over eight hours won't impress your college friends, unless you happen to be 100 years old. The 2011 Toronto Waterfront Marathon wasn't the first world record for Fauja Singh (the "Punjabi Tornado"). He was the fastest male to run 5,000 meters and 3,000 meters for the over-100 crowd. Not surprisingly, he took his first split in Toronto at little more than a toddler's totter. At mile 18, he stopped for some tea and a rubdown. When the turbaned vegetarian crossed the finish line, he said only, "Anything worth doing is going to be difficult."

No kidding. Yet at 100, why does anyone bother with the ambitions of a younger person? Singh wasn't trying to recapture past glories; he'd never run competitively until he was in his 80s. His six children had grown and married; his wife had passed. One evening in 1994, a fierce Punjabi monsoon storm ripped a sheet of corrugated metal off the roof of a building and decapitated his son, with whom he lived. It was a turning point. Singh began to run as a way of dealing with his grief. It's hard to believe that there are people today who still believe running is pointless, even silly: lots of distance, no destination. But like life itself, running is its own reward.

Just ask Sim Jae-duk. The 44-year-old South Korean ultra-distance runner has completed at least 210 marathons since 1995, finishing all but three of them in less than three hours. He's not fast enough for world records, but then, he's just happy to be alive. A shipbuilder for Daewoo Shipbuilding and Marine Engineering, he spent six years working inside vessels, breathing chemicals and dust through a face mask. By 1993, his respiratory system had so compromised that surgery was recommended. Mr. Sim refused. "Instead of surgery," he says, "I decided to run . . . even if I died, I would die running, with my lungs full of air." His lung capacity in 2003 was about 70 percent; today it's normal. He runs at least three marathons a month, and as many as seven. He's become a celebrity in his native country. Few of us would earnestly say that we run for our lives. But as Mr. Sim demonstrates, in one way or another, we all do. The mortal stakes are just details.

Still, running is a test, a reminder, and the perfect proof that mortality amounts to more than just a pulse. Born with a congenital scarred liver, runner Tom Krumenacker grew up under constant medical supervision. Suffering near chronic internal bleeding, it became clear he needed a liver transplant. His sister-in-law, Heather Walsh, shared his blood type and proved to be a matching donor. She didn't hesitate. On the night of their surgeries, Krumenacker made Heather promise that she'd run a marathon if they both lived. She hated exercise, had never trained for anything, and thought he was crazy. She took longer to heal than expected because the remaining 60 percent of her liver had to regenerate. But when her birthday rolled around in 2005, she opened Krumenacker's card and found that he'd entered them both in the San Diego Rock 'n' Roll Marathon. In training for it, she became a dedicated runner for marathons, half marathons, and triathlons. In giving away living tissue, she gained new life.

Even if running can save your flesh, can it save your soul? Does your life have a second act? Caleb Daniloff was a drunk, a drug addict, and a self-described jerk. Author of *Running Ransom Road*, he chronicles a rebirth that psychotherapy, Alcoholics Anonymous, and the love of family and friends couldn't bring him. In an essay, he writes, "When I finally came to after 15 years of chronic drinking, I was enveloped by the ultimate hangover. Not, what did I do last night? But, who was I for the last decade?" So Daniloff started running.

As he notes in his book, new life doesn't slay the ghosts of your past: "I don't wake up hung over anymore, but I do sometimes wake up haunted—by who I used to be, by the people I've done wrong. On the days I don't run, it's worse. I'm filled with a different kind of thirst, a need to move between places—across bridges, over water, over city lines. . . . The hard work of the run fortifies my will."

**—Marty Jerome** ■

# January

| SUNDAY | MONDAY | TUESDAY | WEDNESDAY | THURSDAY | FRIDAY | SATURDAY |
|--------|--------|---------|-----------|----------|--------|----------|
| | | | | **1**<br><br>New Year's Day<br>Kwanzaa ends (USA) | **2**<br><br>New Year's Day<br>(observed) (NZ)<br>Bank Holiday (UK—Scotland) | **3** |
| **4** | **5** | **6** | **7** | **8** | **9** | **10** |
| **11** | **12** | **13** | **14** | **15** | **16** | **17** |
| **18** | **19**<br><br>Martin Luther King Jr.'s<br>Birthday (observed) (USA) | **20** | **21** | **22** | **23** | **24** |
| **25** | **26**<br><br>Australia Day | **27** | **28** | **29** | **30** | **31** |

*"Life begins as the end of your comfort zone."*

—Neale Donald Walsch, author of *Conversations with God*

# GAMBLER

You'd have to believe that a runner is just as likely to visit a casino, bid into the office Super Bowl pool, or buy a lottery ticket as anyone else. Yet taking stakes with money should seem trivial, even dull, every time you lace up your running shoes.

Of course, getting out of bed in the morning is a gamble, even if it doesn't spike the same psychological charge a card player feels with a great or terrible hand. We make bets throughout our lives, throughout the day—with our jobs, our relationships, our daily commute. By comparison, workouts bring seemingly risk-free comfort in their familiarity and in the expansive ways they grow us as athletes and as human beings. We trust that the benefits of training are abundant and endless.

This is an illusion. Familiarity will take us down, even though it's an essential part of training. Knowing when knees and hams are sufficiently warmed up to begin harder work; understanding what a hill will demand; recognizing the difference between fatigue and injury—this is indispensable knowledge to any runner, and only personal experience can provide it. Yet danger lies in the lull of routine. The repetitive nature of workouts, of running itself, reassures us that we will always improve. But the magic eventually tapers or stops. House wins.

All runners should periodically raise their stakes, not necessarily with greater mileage or faster speeds, but with unfamiliar challenges that shed new light into untapped abilities and unacknowledged deficiencies. Racing is the usual raise and call. Its power for organizing a training program is breathtaking. The gamble is that, whether you succeed or fail at your goals for any event, your running shoes are staring at you the day afterward. Adrenaline and hopeful desire are depleted, and unless you have another race date circled on the calendar, your training program may simply collapse. You have to plan for this in advance.

Many runners move their training programs laterally. Trail running is great fun so long as you don't bring the conceits of a street runner to the game. You have to go slower and develop new skills, especially about where your eyes fall. Also, you will need new shoes. Likewise, track and cross training bring new challenges, new uncertainties (and new aches and injuries). But they can also make you a better runner.

As you plan how to raise your game in the coming year, be keenly aware of what you've already got riding on the table, especially your emotional stakes. Successive defeats make many runners call it quits for good. Overdependence on a running partner or a group can sabotage your training program if these people suddenly vanish. You rarely consider the psychological toll an extended injury takes until one sidelines you. The disappointments from an aging body are laid bare with a runner. The good news is that training slows this inevitable decline. Better still, it not only extends your life; training enriches it. You can bet on it. ∎

**Distance carried forward:** _____

# 29 Monday
_____
_____
_____

**Where & When:** _____ **Distance:** _____

**Comments:** _____
_____

# 30 Tuesday
_____
_____
_____

**Where & When:** _____ **Distance:** _____

**Comments:** _____
_____

# 31 Wednesday
_____
_____
_____

**Where & When:** _____ **Distance:** _____

**Comments:** _____
_____

# 1 Thursday                                                                    1
_____
_____
_____

**Where & When:** _____ **Distance:** _____

**Comments:** _____
_____

# 2 Friday                                                                      2
_____
_____
_____

**Where & When:** _____ **Distance:** _____

**Comments:** _____
_____

# Dec 2014/Jan

**Saturday 3**

3

Where & When: _____  Distance: _____
Comments: _____

**Sunday 4**

4

Where & When: _____  Distance: _____
Comments: _____

© Bob Allen/gettyimages

**tip:** The faster way to raise your mileage isn't by adding miles to your current workout. Instead, add an extra workout to your routine each week.

Distance this week: _____  Weight: _____

**Distance carried forward:** _____

## 5 Monday                                                          5

_____

_____

**Where & When:** _____ **Distance:** _____

**Comments:** _____

## 6 Tuesday                                                         6

_____

_____

**Where & When:** _____ **Distance:** _____

**Comments:** _____

## 7 Wednesday                                                       7

_____

_____

**Where & When:** _____ **Distance:** _____

**Comments:** _____

## 8 Thursday                                                        8

_____

_____

**Where & When:** _____ **Distance:** _____

**Comments:** _____

## 9 Friday                                                          9

_____

_____

**Where & When:** _____ **Distance:** _____

**Comments:** _____

# January

**10**

Where & When: _____          Distance: _____

Comments: _____

**11**

Where & When: _____          Distance: _____

Comments: _____

© Klaus Vedfelt/gettyimages

**tip:** Walk downhill in workouts. Uphill sprints put less stress on joints and muscles with each foot strike.

**Distance this week:** _____          **Weight:** _____

**Distance carried forward:** _____

## 12 Monday                                                    12

_____

_____

_____

Where & When: _____    Distance: _____

Comments: _____

_____

## 13 Tuesday                                                   13

_____

_____

_____

Where & When: _____    Distance: _____

Comments: _____

_____

## 14 Wednesday                                                 14

_____

_____

_____

Where & When: _____    Distance: _____

Comments: _____

_____

## 15 Thursday                                                  15

_____

_____

_____

Where & When: _____    Distance: _____

Comments: _____

_____

## 16 Friday                                                    16

_____

_____

_____

Where & When: _____    Distance: _____

Comments: _____

_____

# January

**Saturday 17**

17

Where & When: | Distance:

Comments:

**Sunday 18**

18

Where & When: | Distance:

Comments:

© John Kelly/gettyimages

**tip:** Psychologically breaking down big goals into smaller efforts sustains motivation.

Distance this week: | Weight:

**Distance carried forward:** _____

# 19 Monday                                                          19
_____
_____
_____

**Where & When:** _____  **Distance:** _____
**Comments:** _____
_____

# 20 Tuesday                                                         20
_____
_____
_____

**Where & When:** _____  **Distance:** _____
**Comments:** _____
_____

# 21 Wednesday                                                       21
_____
_____
_____

**Where & When:** _____  **Distance:** _____
**Comments:** _____
_____

# 22 Thursday                                                        22
_____
_____
_____

**Where & When:** _____  **Distance:** _____
**Comments:** _____
_____

# 23 Friday                                                          23
_____
_____
_____

**Where & When:** _____  **Distance:** _____
**Comments:** _____
_____

24

## Saturday 24

Where & When: _____  Distance: _____

Comments: _____

25

## Sunday 25

Where & When: _____  Distance: _____

Comments: _____

© Gene Chutka/gettyimages

**tip:** Do your rest days make you restless? So run seven days a week. Just go very easy on every other workout.

Distance this week: _____  Weight: _____

**Distance carried forward:** _____

# 26 Monday 26
_____
_____
_____

**Where & When:** _____ **Distance:** _____
**Comments:** _____
_____

# 27 Tuesday 27
_____
_____
_____

**Where & When:** _____ **Distance:** _____
**Comments:** _____
_____

# 28 Wednesday 28
_____
_____
_____

**Where & When:** _____ **Distance:** _____
**Comments:** _____
_____

# 29 Thursday 29
_____
_____
_____

**Where & When:** _____ **Distance:** _____
**Comments:** _____
_____

# 30 Friday 30
_____
_____
_____

**Where & When:** _____ **Distance:** _____
**Comments:** _____
_____

# January/February

**Saturday 31**

_____

_____

_____

**Where & When:** _____ **Distance:** _____
**Comments:** _____

_____

**Sunday 1**

_____

_____

_____

**Where & When:** _____ **Distance:** _____
**Comments:** _____

_____

*"If we can recognize that change and uncertainty are basic principles, we can greet the future and the transformation we are undergoing with the understanding that we do not know enough to be pessimistic."*
—Hazel Henderson, futurist and syndicated columnist

**tip:** You're less likely to overeat when ordering from a menu that lists the amount of brisk walking required to burn off a dish than from a menu that lists calories alone.

Notes: _____

_____

_____

_____

_____

**Distance this week:** _____ **Weight:** _____

# February

| SUNDAY | MONDAY | TUESDAY | WEDNESDAY | THURSDAY | FRIDAY | SATURDAY |
|--------|--------|---------|-----------|----------|--------|----------|
| 1 | 2 | 3 | 4 | 5 | 6 Waitangi Day (NZ) | 7 |
| 8 | 9 | 10 | 11 | 12 | 13 | 14 St. Valentine's Day |
| 15 | 16 Presidents' Day (USA) | 17 | 18 Ash Wednesday | 19 | 20 | 21 |
| 22 | 23 | 24 | 25 | 26 | 27 | 28 |
| | | | | | | |

*"You are imperfect, permanently and inevitably flawed. And you are beautiful."*

—Amy Bloom, American novelist

# VANITY

If the bathroom mirror is your greatest motivator, graciously accept its encouragement. Just don't let it become a tyrant.

Buffed and beautiful runners often hide feint embarrassment about the superficial benefits of training. Many tell fibs about it ("I run to keep my cholesterol in check," you'll hear, even when you know perfectly well it's to sculpt their bums, to flatten their tummies). It's an unnecessary charade. Millions of runners begin through vanity, but discover an elevated sense of well-being, the satisfaction from competition, reduced stress, or their doctor's approval. The benefits cascade. The experience deepens.

Running is the most popular way to control weight in America—as much because of its efficacy as anything else. You get more dramatic results for the time you invest than you'll get from low-impact training. It's not entirely clear why. Swimming, bicycling, and aerobics machines certainly burn calories at an accelerated rate (and like running, continue burning them after the workout has ended). But they require equipment or facilities. And, hour for hour, they won't shed weight as fast as running will. Power walking provides the same cardiovascular conditioning as running, even though it requires roughly twice the time to do it. And even then, it won't hastily melt away pounds.

Fact is, being fit and being slender are not the same things. This recognition too often dooms a training program. Weight control is a complicated business. Muscle weighs more than fat, so it's not uncommon to gain pounds as you get stronger. Running spikes your appetite, which can bound ahead of the calories your workouts burn. Worse, hunger can take weeks to abate when you're sidelined by injury or a lack of motivation. You lose muscle mass as you age and your body redistributes fat in often unflattering ways. Your metabolism changes through the seasons and through the years. For a variety of reasons, your weight is always in flux.

On the other hand, running tones muscle in ways not reported by your impertinent bathroom scale. When combined with resistance exercises and a sensible diet, pounds eventually melt away. All human bodies respond to the training effect, but they advance at different rates and in different ways. Experimentation and persistence will eventually win you results.

They just may not be as dramatic as you'd like. Making peace with your body in the first place is paramount. Those who run purely for the sake of appearance rarely stick with it. The best training programs incorporate a variety of goals. These should change over time, based on the results you get—and those you don't. Critically overweight runners should put hypertension, diabetes, joint stress, and cholesterol over admiring glances from strangers. In other words, it's okay to be pleased with the body that running gives you. Just be pleased with it in as many ways as you can. ■

**Distance carried forward:** _____

## 2 Monday                                              33

_____

_____

_____

**Where & When:** _____  **Distance:** _____

**Comments:** _____

_____

## 3 Tuesday                                             34

_____

_____

_____

**Where & When:** _____  **Distance:** _____

**Comments:** _____

_____

## 4 Wednesday                                           35

_____

_____

_____

**Where & When:** _____  **Distance:** _____

**Comments:** _____

_____

## 5 Thursday                                            36

_____

_____

_____

**Where & When:** _____  **Distance:** _____

**Comments:** _____

_____

## 6 Friday                                              37

_____

_____

_____

**Where & When:** _____  **Distance:** _____

**Comments:** _____

_____

# February

## Saturday 7

38

Where & When:                                    Distance:

Comments:

## Sunday 8

39

Where & When:                                    Distance:

Comments:

© Jordan Siemens/gettyimages

**tip:** Physiological responses to exercise vary wildly between individuals. So don't blame yourself if your running partner is getting fitter, faster, or losing more weight than you while training at the same rate.

**Distance this week:**                           **Weight:**

**Distance carried forward:** _____

## 9 Monday 40
_____
_____
_____

**Where & When:** _____ **Distance:** _____
**Comments:** _____
_____

## 10 Tuesday 41
_____
_____
_____

**Where & When:** _____ **Distance:** _____
**Comments:** _____
_____

## 11 Wednesday 42
_____
_____
_____

**Where & When:** _____ **Distance:** _____
**Comments:** _____
_____

## 12 Thursday 43
_____
_____
_____

**Where & When:** _____ **Distance:** _____
**Comments:** _____
_____

## 13 Friday 44
_____
_____
_____

**Where & When:** _____ **Distance:** _____
**Comments:** _____
_____

# February

## Saturday 14

**45**

_____

_____

_____

**Where & When:** _____  **Distance:** _____

**Comments:** _____

_____

## Sunday 15

**46**

_____

_____

_____

**Where & When:** _____  **Distance:** _____

**Comments:** _____

_____

© Noah Clayton/gettyimages

**tip:** Exercising on an empty stomach does not burn fat faster.

**Distance this week:** _____  **Weight:** _____

**Distance carried forward:**

# 16 Monday 47

Where & When:            Distance:

Comments:

# 17 Tuesday 48

Where & When:            Distance:

Comments:

# 18 Wednesday 49

Where & When:            Distance:

Comments:

# 19 Thursday 50

Where & When:            Distance:

Comments:

# 20 Friday 51

Where & When:            Distance:

Comments:

# February

## Saturday 21

52

Where & When:        Distance:

Comments:

## Sunday 22

53

Where & When:        Distance:

Comments:

© George Rose/gettyimages

**tip:** An easy workout after a big meal burns calories and aids digestion.

Distance this week:        Weight:

**Distance carried forward:** _____

## 23 Monday                                                    54

_____
_____
_____

**Where & When:** _____     **Distance:** _____
**Comments:** _____
_____

## 24 Tuesday                                                   55

_____
_____
_____

**Where & When:** _____     **Distance:** _____
**Comments:** _____
_____

## 25 Wednesday                                                 56

_____
_____
_____

**Where & When:** _____     **Distance:** _____
**Comments:** _____
_____

## 26 Thursday                                                  57

_____
_____
_____

**Where & When:** _____     **Distance:** _____
**Comments:** _____
_____

## 27 Friday                                                    58

_____
_____
_____

**Where & When:** _____     **Distance:** _____
**Comments:** _____
_____

**59** _____ **Saturday 28**

_____
_____
_____

**Where & When:** _____ **Distance:** _____
**Comments:** _____
_____

**60** _____ **Sunday 1**

_____
_____
_____

**Where & When:** _____ **Distance:** _____
**Comments:** _____
_____

*"The great thing in this world is not so much where we stand, as in what direction we are moving."*
—Oliver Wendell Holmes

**tip:** At least one study suggests that resveratrol, a compound in red wine that is believed to benefit heart health for its antioxidant properties, seems to undermine the cardiovascular benefits of exercise.

Notes: _____
_____
_____
_____
_____

**Distance this week:** _____ **Weight:** _____

# March

| SUNDAY | MONDAY | TUESDAY | WEDNESDAY | THURSDAY | FRIDAY | SATURDAY |
|---|---|---|---|---|---|---|
| 1<br><br>St. David's Day (UK) | 2<br><br>Labour Day (Australia—WA) | 3 | 4 | 5<br><br>Purim* | 6 | 7 |
| 8<br><br>International Women's Day | 9<br><br>Eight Hours Day (Australia—TAS)<br>Canberra Day (Australia—ACT)<br>Labour Day (Australia—VIC)<br>Commonwealth Day (Australia, Canada, NZ, UK) | 10 | 11 | 12 | 13 | 14 |
| 15<br><br>Mothering Sunday (Ireland, UK) | 16 | 17<br><br>St. Patrick's Day | 18 | 19 | 20 | 21 |
| 22 | 23 | 24 | 25 | 26 | 27 | 28 |
| 29<br><br>Palm Sunday | 30 | 31 | | | | |

*Begins at sundown the previous day

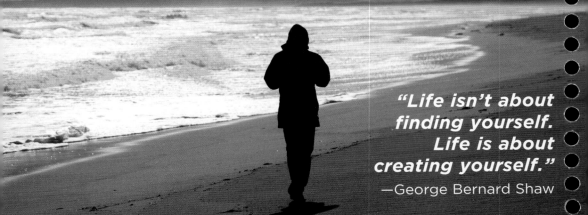

"Life isn't about finding yourself. Life is about creating yourself."
—George Bernard Shaw

# CLERGY

Personal trainers, like preachers, have fluid job descriptions and often, dubious credentials. Their greatest talents work as much from the force of personality as from any formal education. Unfortunately, the corrupt and incompetent in both professions prey on countless suckers and victims.

This isn't to disparage the many advantages a trainer or running coach (or minister) can offer. Elite athletes wouldn't begin a workout unless under a coach's critical gaze. You will always hear effusive anecdotes from fellow runners about the gains a trainer has helped them attain. They can be invaluable for helping a runner recover from an injury. And they fill many roles: an expert, a scold, a confidant, a motivator, a slave driver, a consoler, a friend.

But this is just the problem. Trainers rarely excel at all of these functions with equal ability. Finding help that suits your specific needs can be a prolonged and expensive journey. It can also invite injury. Forthcoming communication is obviously the first step, but your running coach can't become your psychotherapist with a single interview. Time and familiarity will reveal whether the chemistry between you works—or doesn't.

When sizing up a running coach, you should be as specific as possible about your goals. And you should have multiple goals. "I want to run the marathon this April," begs your trainer to become a dream weaver. "I want to run the marathon this April in under three hours," gives her something to work with. It's the same with speed and weight-loss goals. Only you can decide what's realistic. Together you will contrive benchmarks of progress and lay the brickwork for a training program to achieve them.

Before you start following orders, have your coach accompany you on your customary run. This will reveal your form and foot strike, your pace, the ways you challenge yourself (and don't), how quickly fatigue sets in, and the many inefficiencies that are holding back progress. Even your changing facial expressions contribute to the wheelbarrow of information that only a workout can deliver. Is your coach paying attention?

When you're both satisfied that you can work together and are ready to concoct a training plan, begin your own plan about when to fire your coach. It seems cynical, but goals are either achieved or they're not. Move on to the next goal, the next coach. Bear in mind that trainers and running coaches have a financial incentive to stay on your payroll (and many have honed the sales skills to convince you). But after a certain point in your progress, you're only throwing away money.

Still, many runners cling to the illusion that by indefinitely working with a professional, they will continue to improve, when in fact, they're just looking for a friend to keep them motivated, oblivious to the many free forms of motivation—from running clubs to the quiet support of family and running partners—that can be had without the ridiculous mysticism often imposed on trainers. Truth is, in worldly progress, coaches and preachers can offer only a little. ■

**Distance carried forward:**

## 2 Monday 61

Where & When:                                   Distance:

Comments:

## 3 Tuesday 62

Where & When:                                   Distance:

Comments:

## 4 Wednesday 63

Where & When:                                   Distance:

Comments:

## 5 Thursday 64

Where & When:                                   Distance:

Comments:

## 6 Friday 65

Where & When:                                   Distance:

Comments:

**66** _____ **Saturday  7**

_____

_____

_____

**Where & When:** _____ **Distance:** _____

**Comments:** _____

_____

**67** _____ **Sunday  8**

_____

_____

_____

**Where & When:** _____ **Distance:** _____

**Comments:** _____

_____

© Christopher Futcher/gettyimages

**tip:** Give back. Volunteer to work a race. It does wonders for your own training motivation.

**Distance this week:** _____ **Weight:** _____

**Distance carried forward:**

## 9 Monday 68

Where & When:                                    Distance:

Comments:

## 10 Tuesday 69

Where & When:                                    Distance:

Comments:

## 11 Wednesday 70

Where & When:                                    Distance:

Comments:

## 12 Thursday 71

Where & When:                                    Distance:

Comments:

## 13 Friday 72

Where & When:                                    Distance:

Comments:

**73** _____

_____

_____

**Where & When:** _____ **Distance:** _____

**Comments:** _____

_____

**74** _____ **Sunday 15**

_____

_____

**Where & When:** _____ **Distance:** _____

**Comments:** _____

_____

© Stockbyte/gettyimages

**tip:** A running partner's greatest motivating power isn't for speed or distance. It's for the frequency of your workouts.

**Distance this week:** _____ **Weight:** _____

**Distance carried forward:**

## 16 Monday
75

Where & When:          Distance:

Comments:

## 17 Tuesday
76

Where & When:          Distance:

Comments:

## 18 Wednesday
77

Where & When:          Distance:

Comments:

## 19 Thursday
78

Where & When:          Distance:

Comments:

## 20 Friday
79

Where & When:          Distance:

Comments:

# March

**Where & When:**              **Distance:**

**Comments:**

**Sunday 22**

81

**Where & When:**              **Distance:**

**Comments:**

© Erik Isakson/gettyimages

**tip:** Even if you resist running with headphones, music immediately before a workout can boost motivation.

**Distance this week:**              **Weight:**

**Distance carried forward:**

# 23 Monday 82

Where & When:                                    Distance:

Comments:

# 24 Tuesday 83

Where & When:                                    Distance:

Comments:

# 25 Wednesday 84

Where & When:                                    Distance:

Comments:

# 26 Thursday 85

Where & When:                                    Distance:

Comments:

# 27 Friday 86

Where & When:                                    Distance:

Comments:

# March

87

Where & When:                                    Distance:

Comments:

88                                               **Sunday 29**

Where & When:                                    Distance:

Comments:

*"By stretching yourself beyond your perceived level of confidence, you accelerate the development of competence."*

—Michael J. Gelb, author, personal development trainer

**tip:** Low blood sugar saps motivation. If you're dithering about whether to go for a run, eat a snack.

Notes:

Distance this week:                              Weight:

# April

| SUNDAY | MONDAY | TUESDAY | WEDNESDAY | THURSDAY | FRIDAY | SATURDAY |
|--------|--------|---------|-----------|----------|--------|----------|
| | | | 1 | 2 | 3 <br><br> Good Friday (Western) | 4 <br><br> Passover* <br> Easter Saturday <br> (Australia—except TAS, WA) |
| 5 <br><br> Easter (Western) | 6 <br><br> Easter Monday (Australia, Canada, Ireland, NZ, UK— except Scotland) | 7 | 8 | 9 | 10 <br><br> Holy Friday (Orthodox) | 11 <br><br> Passover ends |
| 12 <br><br> Easter (Orthodox) | 13 | 14 | 15 | 16 | 17 | 18 |
| 19 | 20 | 21 | 22 <br><br> Earth Day | 23 <br><br> St. George's Day (UK) | 24 | 25 <br><br> Anzac Day (NZ, Australia) |
| 26 | 27 <br><br> Anzac Day (observed) (Australia—WA) | 28 | 29 | 30 | | |

*Begins at sundown the previous day

"Take care of your body. It's the only place you have to live."

—Jim Rohn, American entrepreneur

# CRIMINALS

Injury is a mugger; defeat a thief. Both rely on ambush—cruel surprise—to take away what's rightfully yours. By contrast, runners are law abiders, dutifully pursuing disciplined training programs, trusting in some higher order that reliably brings reassurance and progress, if not miracles. All is well until some thug lunges from the shadows. As any cop will tell you, the best way to fight crime is to prevent it.

Few of us pay sufficient attention to prevention. Rest is your best protection against injury, of course. But did you know that both elite athletes and beginners require more days off than experienced mid-rangers? All runners should dramatically reduce mileage, or lay off altogether for a week or two, at least twice a year. Competitive runners need even more down time. Easy days should be easy; this requires just as much attention as a day of hill charges. Too often we zone out in a comfort level of effort, only to discover that we've worked a recovery day too hard.

Speaking of recovery, plan it before you put on your running shoes. Certainly, it should incorporate a proper warm-down and perhaps stretching. It should go further. A post-workout nap is not indulgent. Sleep deprivation, in general, can compromise cardiovascular performance by up to 20 percent. Recovery meals should not be concocted while standing at the open refrigerator door, hunger teeming. You'll get more from your training program if you dissociate from your workout after it has ended. Stupid television, wallowing over a massage roller while listening to music, coffee with a friend—whatever—take a quick inventory of the run just completed, then change gears. Whatever went right or wrong, another workout awaits.

Do you have the right defenses against assailants? Strength training makes tough bones and shores up supporting muscles rarely used in your daily workouts, but which can spare twisted ankles and wrenched knees over unexpectedly slippery terrain or sudden evasion maneuvers. It also reduces factors that contribute to overuse injuries. Hydration should begin at least one hour before your run, and if you don't carry water with you, know the park fountains or other places you can tank up. Performance begins to decrease after only a 2 percent loss in body water. And dire trouble lurks in the shadows of dehydration. Periodically renew your attention to attire, foremost in decent running shoes, but also hats, sunglasses, layers of warmth and wicking, sunscreen, even underwear. Crooks work best in overlooked details.

Defeat, competitive and otherwise, is an entirely different sort of crime because it cheats you out of your dreams. Usually you have only yourself to blame, either through lack of preparation or over-ambition, and you won't serve yourself in blaming culprits. Take it as a bitter learning moment, no less than the humiliation of restoring credit cards, identification, and whatnot when you've had your wallet filched. The key is to prevent it from happening again. In other words, don't become your own repeat offender. ■

**Distance carried forward:** _____

## 30 Monday                                                              89

_____

_____

_____

**Where & When:** _____ **Distance:** _____

**Comments:** _____

_____

## 31 Tuesday                                                             90

_____

_____

_____

**Where & When:** _____ **Distance:** _____

**Comments:** _____

_____

## 1 Wednesday                                                            91

_____

_____

_____

**Where & When:** _____ **Distance:** _____

**Comments:** _____

_____

## 2 Thursday                                                             92

_____

_____

_____

**Where & When:** _____ **Distance:** _____

**Comments:** _____

_____

## 3 Friday                                                               93

_____

_____

_____

**Where & When:** _____ **Distance:** _____

**Comments:** _____

_____

**94** _____

_____

_____

_____

**Where & When:** _____ **Distance:** _____

**Comments:** _____

_____

**95** _____ **Sunday 5**

_____

_____

_____

**Where & When:** _____ **Distance:** _____

**Comments:** _____

_____

© altrendo images/gettyimages

**tip:** It's okay to run with a mild sprain. Just keep your effort to a very low level—and have ice on hand when the workout is over.

**Distance this week:** _____ **Weight:** _____

**Distance carried forward:**

## 6 Monday 96

Where & When:                              Distance:

Comments:

## 7 Tuesday 97

Where & When:                              Distance:

Comments:

## 8 Wednesday 98

Where & When:                              Distance:

Comments:

## 9 Thursday 99

Where & When:                              Distance:

Comments:

## 10 Friday 100

Where & When:                              Distance:

Comments:

101 **Saturday 11**

_____

_____

_____

**Where & When:** _____ **Distance:** _____

**Comments:** _____

_____

102 **Sunday 12**

_____

_____

_____

**Where & When:** _____ **Distance:** _____

**Comments:** _____

_____

© MichaelSvoboda/gettyimages

**tip:** Most emergency-room visits for running injuries aren't necessary. Ice, bandages, and nonsteroidal anti-inflammatory drugs at home are typically all the medicine you need. Also, you need plenty of time to heal.

**Distance this week:** _____ **Weight:** _____

**Distance carried forward:** _____

# 13 Monday                                                          103
_____
_____
_____

**Where & When:** _____  **Distance:** _____
**Comments:** _____
_____

# 14 Tuesday                                                         104
_____
_____
_____

**Where & When:** _____  **Distance:** _____
**Comments:** _____
_____

# 15 Wednesday                                                       105
_____
_____
_____

**Where & When:** _____  **Distance:** _____
**Comments:** _____
_____

# 16 Thursday                                                        106
_____
_____
_____

**Where & When:** _____  **Distance:** _____
**Comments:** _____
_____

# 17 Friday                                                          107
_____
_____
_____

**Where & When:** _____  **Distance:** _____
**Comments:** _____
_____

**108** _____

_____

_____

**Where & When:** _____ **Distance:** _____

**Comments:** _____

_____

**109** _____ **Sunday 19**

_____

_____

**Where & When:** _____ **Distance:** _____

**Comments:** _____

_____

© Jordan Siemens/gettyimages

**tip:** If an ache subsides within 10 minutes of a workout and stops entirely after a day or two, it's probably not an injury.

**Distance this week:** _____ **Weight:** _____

**Distance carried forward:**

## 20 Monday                                                    110

Where & When:                               Distance:

Comments:

## 21 Tuesday                                                   111

Where & When:                               Distance:

Comments:

## 22 Wednesday                                                 112

Where & When:                               Distance:

Comments:

## 23 Thursday                                                  113

Where & When:                               Distance:

Comments:

## 24 Friday                                                    114

Where & When:                               Distance:

Comments:

**115**

**Where & When:** _____  **Distance:** _____

**Comments:** _____

**116**

**Sunday 26**

**Where & When:** _____  **Distance:** _____

**Comments:** _____

© 4FR/gettyimages

**tip:** Weight and resistance workouts help prevent stress fractures.

**Distance this week:** _____  **Weight:** _____

**Distance carried forward:** _____

# 27 Monday 117
_____
_____
_____

**Where & When:** _____ **Distance:** _____
**Comments:** _____
_____

# 28 Tuesday 118
_____
_____
_____

**Where & When:** _____ **Distance:** _____
**Comments:** _____
_____

# 29 Wednesday 119
_____
_____
_____

**Where & When:** _____ **Distance:** _____
**Comments:** _____
_____

# 30 Thursday 120
_____
_____
_____

**Where & When:** _____ **Distance:** _____
**Comments:** _____
_____

# 1 Friday 121
_____
_____
_____

**Where & When:** _____ **Distance:** _____
**Comments:** _____
_____

122 _____ **Saturday 2**

_____

_____

_____

**Where & When:** _____  **Distance:** _____
**Comments:** _____

_____

123 _____ **Sunday 3**

_____

_____

**Where & When:** _____  **Distance:** _____
**Comments:** _____

_____

*"Negotiating a marathon requires many of the same mental characteristics needed in life. You have to control your emotions at times, activate your motivation when you're down, and develop resiliency in the face of difficult conditions."*

—Jeff Brown, cognitive-behavioral psychologist, author of *The Winner's Brain*

**tip:** Aging runners often suffer failing knees. Squats strengthen them.

Notes: _____

_____

_____

_____

_____

**Distance this week:** _____  **Weight:** _____

# May

| SUNDAY | MONDAY | TUESDAY | WEDNESDAY | THURSDAY | FRIDAY | SATURDAY |
|---|---|---|---|---|---|---|
| | | | | | 1 | 2 |
| 3 | 4<br><br>May Day (Australia—NT)<br>Early May Bank Holiday<br>(Ireland, UK) | 5 | 6 | 7 | 8 | 9 |
| 10<br><br>Mother's Day<br>(USA, Australia, Canada, NZ) | 11 | 12 | 13 | 14 | 15 | 16<br><br>Armed Forces Day (USA) |
| 17 | 18<br><br>Victoria Day (Canada) | 19 | 20 | 21 | 22 | 23 |
| 24<br>31 | 25<br><br>Memorial Day (USA)<br>Spring Bank Holiday (UK) | 26 | 27 | 28 | 29 | 30 |

*"Courage is fear that has said its prayers."*

—Dorothy Bernard

# SUBMIT

Fight your body all you like, but it will eventually win. In this sense, training is a paradox. We willfully reshape ourselves in ways our bodies naturally resist. The results are gratifying, sometimes breathtaking. Trouble lurks when willfulness overtakes reason. Too often, it's our goals that are out of whack.

This is how the miracle of the training effect loses its luster. Some people simply shouldn't run marathons (some shouldn't run at all). No one likes to hear these things, but there you have it. We are each unique in our morph, metabolism, running form, muscle mass, cardiovascular capacity, and the rate to which we respond to training. All of these are improved with a consistent and progressive workout regime. Still, you can't transform a tortoise into a hare.

So running goals should acknowledge your inherent limitations as well as your talents. All runners should periodically reassess their abilities for speed— and continually build on them. Just bear in mind that distance or trail-running goals may better suit the equipment birth gave you.

It's the same with weight loss. Countless running programs are abandoned each year from abject frustration: Your trim running partner clocks the identical mileage and pace as you, yet these workouts somehow fail to trim your fanny, dispatch your paunch. There's no quibbling that running plays a powerful role in managing weight. But your metabolism is unique. Eventually, you'll have to make peace with yourself.

Also, patience helps. Though the training effect is universal, every runner responds to it in inimitable ways. Some runners seem to accrue both strength and endurance overnight. For others, it builds like interest in a cheap checking account—or muscle mass excels faster than cardio base. Further complicating matters, we all suffer dispiriting and mysterious plateaus and valleys on the road to improvement. Three weeks of steady progress yields to plodding, painful setbacks, seemingly for no reason. Don't overanalyze these periods; every runner has them. Persistence will eventually put you back on track.

It won't, however, help you fight age or injury, both of which are rolling snowballs. The most common mistake a runner makes is returning to normal workouts before an injury is sufficiently healed, begging for relapse. Recurring injuries tend to accumulate. It's far wiser to adjust goals than to put faith in blind determination. No less, you can't run back into the arms of your youth and only fools make the attempt. Lose the judgment about downsizing your goals as you age. Just seek different opportunities.

This is the psychological miracle of the training effect. Running forces us to see unvarnished truths about who we are, our strengths and limitations, our misplaced desires and untapped potential with every workout. There's no need to run away from what greets us in the mirror. ∎

**Distance carried forward:** _____

## 4 Monday                                                        124

_____
_____
_____

**Where & When:** _____ **Distance:** _____
**Comments:** _____
_____

## 5 Tuesday                                                       125

_____
_____
_____

**Where & When:** _____ **Distance:** _____
**Comments:** _____
_____

## 6 Wednesday                                                     126

_____
_____
_____

**Where & When:** _____ **Distance:** _____
**Comments:** _____
_____

## 7 Thursday                                                      127

_____
_____
_____

**Where & When:** _____ **Distance:** _____
**Comments:** _____
_____

## 8 Friday                                                        128

_____
_____
_____

**Where & When:** _____ **Distance:** _____
**Comments:** _____
_____

# May

**129**

_____
_____
_____

**Where & When:** _____  **Distance:** _____
**Comments:** _____
_____

**130**

**Sunday 10**

_____
_____
_____

**Where & When:** _____  **Distance:** _____
**Comments:** _____
_____

© Andrew Rich/gettyimages

**tip:** Worried that you'll lose your nerve for your first race? Tell everyone you know you're running it. You'll be held accountable.

**Distance this week:** _____  **Weight:** _____

**Distance carried forward:** _____

## 11 Monday _____ 131
_____
_____
_____

**Where & When:** _____ **Distance:** _____
**Comments:** _____
_____

## 12 Tuesday _____ 132
_____
_____
_____

**Where & When:** _____ **Distance:** _____
**Comments:** _____
_____

## 13 Wednesday _____ 133
_____
_____
_____

**Where & When:** _____ **Distance:** _____
**Comments:** _____
_____

## 14 Thursday _____ 134
_____
_____
_____

**Where & When:** _____ **Distance:** _____
**Comments:** _____
_____

## 15 Friday _____ 135
_____
_____
_____

**Where & When:** _____ **Distance:** _____
**Comments:** _____

# May

**Where & When:**            **Distance:**

**Comments:**

**Where & When:**            **Distance:**

**Comments:**

© beyond foto/gettyimages

**tip:** Despite the persistent myth, a warm-down won't decrease soreness or increase how limber you are. However, it may provide a gentle post-workout landing for your heart.

**Distance this week:**            **Weight:**

**Distance carried forward:** _____

# 18 Monday                                                           138

_____
_____
_____

**Where & When:** _____ **Distance:** _____
**Comments:** _____
_____

# 19 Tuesday                                                          139

_____
_____
_____

**Where & When:** _____ **Distance:** _____
**Comments:** _____
_____

# 20 Wednesday                                                        140

_____
_____
_____

**Where & When:** _____ **Distance:** _____
**Comments:** _____
_____

# 21 Thursday                                                         141

_____
_____
_____

**Where & When:** _____ **Distance:** _____
**Comments:** _____
_____

# 22 Friday                                                           142

_____
_____
_____

**Where & When:** _____ **Distance:** _____
**Comments:** _____
_____

# May

## Saturday 23

143

Where & When: _____  Distance: _____

Comments: _____

## Sunday 24

144

Where & When: _____  Distance: _____

Comments: _____

© Randall Levensaler/gettyimages

**tip:** For a good night's sleep, work out well ahead of bed time, eat dinner at the same hour each night, avoid caffeine after 4:00 p.m., and keep your bedroom temperature constant.

**Distance this week:** _____  **Weight:** _____

**Distance carried forward:**

## 25 Monday 145

Where & When:                                    Distance:

Comments:

## 26 Tuesday 146

Where & When:                                    Distance:

Comments:

## 27 Wednesday 147

Where & When:                                    Distance:

Comments:

## 28 Thursday 148

Where & When:                                    Distance:

Comments:

## 29 Friday 149

Where & When:                                    Distance:

Comments:

**150**

Where & When: _____ Distance: _____

Comments: _____

**151**

Where & When: _____ Distance: _____

Comments: _____

*"Sometimes a breakdown can be the beginning of a kind of breakthrough, a way of living in advance through a trauma that prepares you for a future of radical transformation."*

—Cherrie Moraga, writer, poet, playwright

**tip:** A higher resting heart rate (above 70 beats per minute) presages a shorter life span—even if you're in shape and healthy.

Notes: _____

_____

_____

_____

Distance this week: _____ Weight: _____

# June

| SUNDAY | MONDAY | TUESDAY | WEDNESDAY | THURSDAY | FRIDAY | SATURDAY |
|---|---|---|---|---|---|---|
| | 1<br><br>Queen's Birthday (NZ)<br>Foundation Day<br>(Australia—WA)<br>Spring Bank Holiday (Ireland) | 2 | 3 | 4 | 5 | 6 |
| 7 | 8<br><br>Queen's Birthday<br>(Australia—except WA) | 9 | 10 | 11 | 12 | 13 |
| 14<br><br>Flag Day (USA) | 15 | 16 | 17 | 18<br><br>Ramadan | 19 | 20 |
| 21<br><br>Father's Day<br>(USA, Canada, Ireland, UK) | 22 | 23 | 24 | 25 | 26 | 27 |
| 28 | 29 | 30 | | | | |

## "Be the change you want to see in the world."
### —Mahatma Gandhi

# PSYCHE

Which is the bigger liar, body or brain? And which is more likely to shore you up at the limit of your abilities, to forestall collapse, to push you onward?

The answer is muddled for sports physiologists, though heaven knows great nerdy attention has served the subject. Fatigue is complicated. Strictly speaking, it's physical, the failure of your muscles to contract, either because they're depleted of glycogen or because your cardiovascular machinery can't pump sufficient oxygen to make them fire. Yet every runner knows that the brain plays lion tamer over this whole business.

The opposite is also true. Nothing clears mental fatigue like a hard workout—after an all-nighter or doing your taxes, a performance, a heated argument with a loved one, or even just endless days of plodding hours at any chore or duty. The first few minutes of a run afterward feel as if a physical weight has been lifted. Then comes a curious freedom; whatever held your mind in play ten minutes ago is now beside the point. Push a little harder, and exhilaration overtakes your effort, and with it comes clarity. A hard run may not save your marriage or lessen the pile of work on your desk, but it quite often clears the head.

Paradoxically, mental fatigue can likewise induce physical exhaustion, even when muscles have plenty of juice in reserve. It has little effect on strength or speed, but a weary mind has been proven to tax endurance. You could almost believe that it orders its own priorities, signaling to your eager legs that they are as tired as it is, so please lay off. It is lying to them. Whatever the physiological explanation, exercise feels harder when your brain is tired. You're more likely to end a workout, to give up on competitive goals in a race. This much scientists can tell us.

Legs fib, too. As physical exhaustion mounts, concentration diffuses. Hitting the proverbial wall in a marathon is as much a psychological, as a physical phenomenon. You're lost. You can't judge whether you have sufficient reserves to make the finish line. Likewise, the first steps that turn leaden in a long workout, especially on an unfamiliar course, telegraph to the brain a false urgency of despair. You feel hopeless.

Feel? Where do emotions enter the picture? Actually, they inform every step of a race or workout, and they're the pivot point where brain and body sometimes reconcile their cheating differences. An overwhelmed runner learns to break down goals, to shove the bigger picture aside. Determination alone can get you to the next bend in the road, to the pine meadow within eyesight, even when you're exhausted. Once you've reached it, you devise another achievable goal, brain and body finally working together.

Emotions—ego, hope, desire, courage, whatever—make a terrible pathway for reaching important goals, competitive or otherwise. Physical preparation and cold-eyed strategy are the better route to success. But feelings matter. Take help anywhere you can get it. ∎

**Distance carried forward:** _____

## 1 Monday                                                         152

_____

_____

**Where & When:** _____     **Distance:** _____

**Comments:** _____

## 2 Tuesday                                                        153

_____

_____

**Where & When:** _____     **Distance:** _____

**Comments:** _____

## 3 Wednesday                                                      154

_____

_____

**Where & When:** _____     **Distance:** _____

**Comments:** _____

## 4 Thursday                                                       155

_____

_____

**Where & When:** _____     **Distance:** _____

**Comments:** _____

## 5 Friday                                                         156

_____

_____

**Where & When:** _____     **Distance:** _____

**Comments:** _____

157

_____
_____
_____

**Where & When:** _____   **Distance:** _____
**Comments:** _____

**Sunday 7**

158 _____

_____
_____
_____

**Where & When:** _____   **Distance:** _____
**Comments:** _____

© amriphoto/gettyimages

**tip:** Runners need extra calcium. Load up on dark, leafy green vegetables, tofu or other soy products, and calcium-fortified foods.

**Distance this week:** _____   **Weight:** _____

**Distance carried forward:**

# 8 Monday 159

Where & When:          Distance:

Comments:

# 9 Tuesday 160

Where & When:          Distance:

Comments:

# 10 Wednesday 161

Where & When:          Distance:

Comments:

# 11 Thursday 162

Where & When:          Distance:

Comments:

# 12 Friday 163

Where & When:          Distance:

Comments:

**164** _____

_____

_____

**Where & When:** _____ **Distance:** _____

**Comments:** _____

_____

**165** _____ **Sunday 14**

_____

_____

**Where & When:** _____ **Distance:** _____

**Comments:** _____

_____

© ZenShui/Alix Minde/gettyimages

**tip:** Running in sand is a great way to build muscles that play supporting roles in your regular run. But keep workouts short.

**Distance this week:** _____ **Weight:** _____

**Distance carried forward:** _____

## 15 Monday                                                          166

_____

_____

_____

**Where & When:** _____ **Distance:** _____

**Comments:** _____

_____

## 16 Tuesday                                                         167

_____

_____

_____

**Where & When:** _____ **Distance:** _____

**Comments:** _____

_____

## 17 Wednesday                                                       168

_____

_____

_____

**Where & When:** _____ **Distance:** _____

**Comments:** _____

_____

## 18 Thursday                                                        169

_____

_____

_____

**Where & When:** _____ **Distance:** _____

**Comments:** _____

_____

## 19 Friday                                                          170

_____

_____

_____

**Where & When:** _____ **Distance:** _____

**Comments:** _____

_____

# June

## Saturday 20

Where & When: _____                     Distance: _____

Comments: _____

## Sunday 21

Where & When: _____                     Distance: _____

Comments: _____

© Andrew Rich/gettyimages

**tip:** Leave the two inner lanes of a track for faster runners.

**Distance this week:** _____                     **Weight:** _____

**Distance carried forward:** _____

## 22 Monday                                                          173

_____

_____

_____

**Where & When:** _____    **Distance:** _____

**Comments:** _____

_____

## 23 Tuesday                                                         174

_____

_____

_____

**Where & When:** _____    **Distance:** _____

**Comments:** _____

_____

## 24 Wednesday                                                       175

_____

_____

_____

**Where & When:** _____    **Distance:** _____

**Comments:** _____

_____

## 25 Thursday                                                        176

_____

_____

_____

**Where & When:** _____    **Distance:** _____

**Comments:** _____

_____

## 26 Friday                                                          177

_____

_____

_____

**Where & When:** _____    **Distance:** _____

**Comments:** _____

_____

**178** <u>Saturday 27</u>

Where & When: Distance:

Comments:

**179** <u>Sunday 28</u>

Where & When: Distance:

Comments:

*"Mind is everything; muscle, mere pieces of rubber. All that I am, I am because of my mind."*

—Paavo Nurmi, Finnish distance runner, who won a record nine Olympic gold medals between 1920 and 1928

**tip:** Energy drinks are no more effective than coffee for boosting your energy. And very few other health claims have actually been tested.

Notes:

Distance this week: Weight:

# July

| SUNDAY | MONDAY | TUESDAY | WEDNESDAY | THURSDAY | FRIDAY | SATURDAY |
|--------|--------|---------|-----------|----------|--------|----------|
| | | | 1<br><br>Canada Day | 2 | 3 | 4<br><br>Independence Day (USA) |
| 5 | 6 | 7 | 8 | 9 | 10 | 11 |
| 12 | 13 | 14 | 15 | 16 | 17 | 18<br><br>Eid al-Fitr |
| 19 | 20 | 21 | 22 | 23 | 24 | 25 |
| 26 | 27 | 28 | 29 | 30 | 31 | |

*"Best is good. Better is best."*
—Lisa Grunwald, American author

# DRAGONS

July is bigger than you are, and probably meaner, too. It's odd how cold-weather months urge us to reorganize our training programs wholesale—retreat to the treadmill, truncate workouts, go lazy in winter's gloom. Yet a runner can easily prevent the twin perils of frigid training, hypothermia and frostbite. Winter presents a sometimes bleak, but relatively harmless, environment to run.

Summer can kill you. Warm weather induces insouciance in runners. We dance around the dragon, fecklessly believing we can stay shy of its wrath. Yet sun stroke, heat exhaustion, and dehydration tend to announce themselves only when it's too late. Hot weather, not cold, should make us revise our training programs in big ways.

Start with mileage. You needn't scale back; in fact, high summer presents the perfect challenge to extend your endurance. Just don't let it get the better of you. Assuming you've acclimated to the heat by running into its embrace gradually from the chilly months (it takes at least two weeks to build up the blood plasma in your system that will keep your body cool), you can begin to add miles, so long you go slowly. Sweltering heat adds a dimension of resistance to any training program, which can turn suddenly dangerous. Again, add miles slowly and be willing to scale back your customary pace. You'll reap the rewards with the first snap of autumn in the air.

Summer's sacrifice is intensity—intervals and other speed drills, hill charges, and the like. Back away from these or stop them entirely. Yes, you'll pay for it in cooler months with the loss of strength and speed. But with a more robust cardio-base and better endurance, you'll be able to reintegrate speed work quickly.

Meanwhile, be inventive. Some runners revile the idea of an early-morning workout when the temperature is coolest and pollution is low. Yet an early-dawn run kick-starts your day with exuberance and satisfaction. It often makes converts for life. Likewise, the long days of summer let you run deep into the evening. If you know a route with sufficient lighting (not just to protect against crime and traffic, but for footing), a midnight run brings an entirely new experience into your training routine. So does a humbling slapdash run in a summer downpour—or trail running, when paths are dry, and you can run alongside a cool body of water or under a canopy of trees. Splitting your workout between morning and dusk lets you escape the enervating tortures of the heat while building muscle at both ends of the day. Make the time for it, and you won't regret it.

But even then, you have to stare down the snarling dragon. Every summer should call into review your heat-fighting arsenal, from hats and eye gear to shorts, shoes, and sunscreen. Central to all of this is hydration. Get in the habit of having a glass of water within reach throughout the day. Heat can be dangerous, but it teems with possibilities. ■

**Distance carried forward:** _____

## 29 Monday                                      180

_____
_____
_____
_____

**Where & When:** _____  **Distance:** _____
**Comments:** _____
_____

## 30 Tuesday                                     181

_____
_____
_____
_____

**Where & When:** _____  **Distance:** _____
**Comments:** _____
_____

## 1 Wednesday                                    182

_____
_____
_____
_____

**Where & When:** _____  **Distance:** _____
**Comments:** _____
_____

## 2 Thursday                                     183

_____
_____
_____
_____

**Where & When:** _____  **Distance:** _____
**Comments:** _____
_____

## 3 Friday                                       184

_____
_____
_____
_____

**Where & When:** _____  **Distance:** _____
**Comments:** _____
_____

# June/July

## Saturday 4

_____

_____

_____

**Where & When:** _____  **Distance:** _____

**Comments:** _____

_____

## Sunday 5

_____

_____

_____

**Where & When:** _____  **Distance:** _____

**Comments:** _____

_____

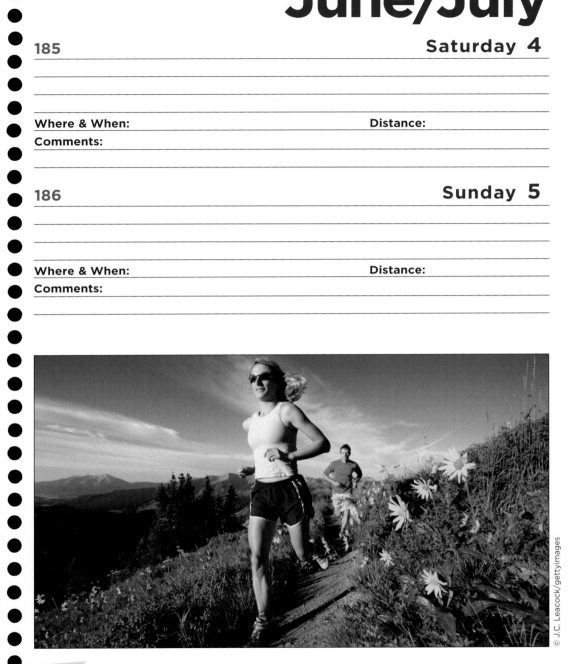

© J.C. Leacock/gettyimages

**tip:** Sunglasses don't just repel glare. They protect your eyes from dust and debris kicked up by cars, the wind, and fate.

**Distance this week:** _____  **Weight:** _____

**Distance carried forward:** _____

## 6 Monday 187

_____
_____
_____

**Where & When:** _____ **Distance:** _____

**Comments:** _____
_____

## 7 Tuesday 188

_____
_____
_____

**Where & When:** _____ **Distance:** _____

**Comments:** _____
_____

## 8 Wednesday 189

_____
_____
_____

**Where & When:** _____ **Distance:** _____

**Comments:** _____
_____

## 9 Thursday 190

_____
_____
_____

**Where & When:** _____ **Distance:** _____

**Comments:** _____
_____

## 10 Friday 191

_____
_____
_____

**Where & When:** _____ **Distance:** _____

**Comments:** _____
_____

# July

## Saturday 11

Where & When: _____ Distance: _____
Comments: _____

## Sunday 12

Where & When: _____ Distance: _____
Comments: _____

© Birgitte Magnus/gettyimages

**tip:** Running is an excellent way to shake jet lag.

Distance this week: _____ Weight: _____

**Distance carried forward:** _____

# 13 Monday                                                                194

_____
_____
_____

**Where & When:** _____          **Distance:** _____
**Comments:** _____
_____

# 14 Tuesday                                                               195

_____
_____
_____

**Where & When:** _____          **Distance:** _____
**Comments:** _____
_____

# 15 Wednesday                                                             196

_____
_____
_____

**Where & When:** _____          **Distance:** _____
**Comments:** _____
_____

# 16 Thursday                                                              197

_____
_____
_____

**Where & When:** _____          **Distance:** _____
**Comments:** _____
_____

# 17 Friday                                                                198

_____
_____
_____

**Where & When:** _____          **Distance:** _____
**Comments:** _____
_____

**Saturday 18**

199

Where & When: _____ Distance: _____

Comments: _____

**Sunday 19**

200

Where & When: _____ Distance: _____

Comments: _____

© Jordan Siemens/gettyimages

**tip:** Growing evidence shows that exercise fights cancer. And it absolutely aids in recovery.

**Distance this week:** _____ **Weight:** _____

**Distance carried forward:** _____

# 20 Monday                                                          201

_____
_____
_____

**Where & When:** _____     **Distance:** _____
**Comments:** _____

_____

# 21 Tuesday                                                         202

_____
_____
_____

**Where & When:** _____     **Distance:** _____
**Comments:** _____

_____

# 22 Wednesday                                                       203

_____
_____
_____

**Where & When:** _____     **Distance:** _____
**Comments:** _____

_____

# 23 Thursday                                                        204

_____
_____
_____

**Where & When:** _____     **Distance:** _____
**Comments:** _____

_____

# 24 Friday                                                          205

_____
_____
_____

**Where & When:** _____     **Distance:** _____
**Comments:** _____

_____

# July

206

**Where & When:**                                        **Distance:**

**Comments:**

207

**Sunday 26**

**Where & When:**                                        **Distance:**

**Comments:**

© stevecoleimages/gettyimages

**tip:** Exercise significantly improves the cognitive abilities and academic performance of children—not to mention their health.

**Distance this week:**                                        **Weight:**

**Distance carried forward:**

## 27 Monday 208

Where & When: Distance:

Comments:

## 28 Tuesday 209

Where & When: Distance:

Comments:

## 29 Wednesday 210

Where & When: Distance:

Comments:

## 30 Thursday 211

Where & When: Distance:

Comments:

## 31 Friday 212

Where & When: Distance:

Comments:

# July/August

**Saturday 1**

_____

**Where & When:** _____ **Distance:** _____

**Comments:** _____

_____

**Sunday 2**

_____

**Where & When:** _____ **Distance:** _____

**Comments:** _____

_____

_"We are not unlike a particularly hardy crustacean. The lobster grows by developing and shedding a series of hard, protective shells. . . . With each passage from one stage of human growth to the next we, too, must shed a protective structure."_
—Gail Sheehy

**tip:** Sugared drinks raise the risks for heart disease.

Notes: _____

_____

_____

_____

_____

**Distance this week:** _____ **Weight:** _____

# August

| SUNDAY | MONDAY | TUESDAY | WEDNESDAY | THURSDAY | FRIDAY | SATURDAY |
|--------|--------|---------|-----------|----------|--------|----------|
| | | | | | | 1 |
| 2 | 3 <br><br> Summer Bank Holiday (Ireland, UK—Scotland, Australia—NSW) <br> Picnic Day (Australia—NT) | 4 | 5 | 6 | 7 | 8 |
| 9 | 10 | 11 | 12 | 13 | 14 | 15 |
| 16 | 17 | 18 | 19 | 20 | 21 | 22 |
| 23 | 24 | 25 | 26 | 27 | 28 | 29 |
| 30 | 31 <br><br> Summer Bank Holiday (UK—except Scotland) | | | | | |

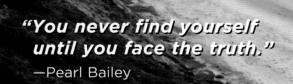

*"You never find yourself until you face the truth."*

—Pearl Bailey

# ACCEPTANCE

The many truths running reveals about your abilities and your character are both bitter and sweet. They confront you on a daily basis, whether in a race or in a solemn workout. So what do you do with this information once you have it?

Ironically, surges of progress are devious, easy to act on, often difficult to untangle. Large or small, they point to new possibilities, new avenues for improvement. They require only a little applied imagination and faith. They lead you to believe in yourself in new ways. Unfortunately, that's how they can turn on you. A three-month burst of advances, your customary mileage growing by unexpected leaps, suddenly holds out the glimmer that you're ready for your first marathon.

When you fail to complete it (or would better measure your time with a calendar than a stopwatch), the demoralization arrives like a punch to the stomach. What went wrong? So it is with any goal for which you overreach, despite accumulated evidence that you've got what it takes to meet it. Danger lies in throwing in the towel in these moments, in believing that the progress you made was all a mirage. Dashed goals almost always overstate your shortcomings. Your advancement as a runner is an essential truth; you've logged the miles, clocked the times, to prove it. Your efforts may need to be redirected, ambitions lowered. But the stupidest thing you can do to your training program is to dismiss your many successes, big or small.

Failure, straight up, is easier to manage. When a work colleague blows by you in the late stage of a race even though he's logged half the miles you have in preparation— or the bathroom scale reports news you'd rather not see—you have to own it. There's no dodging the truth and rationalization is a coward's retreat. Find the humility to face the mean facts. Then resolve to beat the stuffing out of them.

Of course, determination alone won't do it. You'll need to bring cold analysis and calculation to the game. More useful, ask why are you doing this in the first place? Running goals should extend only slightly—realistically—ahead of your abilities. Workouts, not wide-eyed imagination, should drive the bus. Sometimes a lateral approach works best. Cross training, dedicated speed work, trail running, twice-daily runs, and extended off days may yield results that elude you through hope and hard work alone. Use failure as a time to experiment, to reassess your abilities, to find new truths about yourself.

These may surprise you. Too often we let discouragement end the effort. One useful strategy is to shorten the timeline for reexamining goals. Break them down. Bring them up for review more frequently. You may discover that you're better suited to shorter, faster competitive events than to endurance races, that weight control is a battle fought on multiple fronts, that cross-country running brings welcome diversion from the monotony of road training. Whether you succeed or fail, build on what you learn. ∎

**Distance carried forward:**

# 3 Monday 215

**Where & When:** **Distance:**

**Comments:**

# 4 Tuesday 216

**Where & When:** **Distance:**

**Comments:**

# 5 Wednesday 217

**Where & When:** **Distance:**

**Comments:**

# 6 Thursday 218

**Where & When:** **Distance:**

**Comments:**

# 7 Friday 219

**Where & When:** **Distance:**

**Comments:**

# August

220

Where & When:                                 Distance:

Comments:

**Sunday 9**

221

Where & When:                                 Distance:

Comments:

© Myles Dumas/gettyimages

**tip:** Space your races—never more than one event every two weeks. Competition takes a physical and psychological toll. It begs for burnout.

Distance this week:                                          Weight:

**Distance carried forward:** _____

# 10 Monday                                                    222

_____
_____
_____

**Where & When:** _____ **Distance:** _____
**Comments:** _____
_____

# 11 Tuesday                                                   223

_____
_____
_____

**Where & When:** _____ **Distance:** _____
**Comments:** _____
_____

# 12 Wednesday                                                 224

_____
_____
_____

**Where & When:** _____ **Distance:** _____
**Comments:** _____
_____

# 13 Thursday                                                  225

_____
_____
_____

**Where & When:** _____ **Distance:** _____
**Comments:** _____
_____

# 14 Friday                                                    226

_____
_____
_____

**Where & When:** _____ **Distance:** _____
**Comments:** _____
_____

**Saturday 15**

227

_____

_____

_____

**Where & When:** _____    **Distance:** _____

**Comments:** _____

_____

**Sunday 16**

228

_____

_____

_____

**Where & When:** _____    **Distance:** _____

**Comments:** _____

_____

© Arthur Kwiatkowski/gettyimages

**tip:** Dirt is cooler than asphalt for radiating ground heat.

**Distance this week:** _____    **Weight:** _____

**Distance carried forward:**

# 17 Monday 229

Where & When:        Distance:

Comments:

# 18 Tuesday 230

Where & When:        Distance:

Comments:

# 19 Wednesday 231

Where & When:        Distance:

Comments:

# 20 Thursday 232

Where & When:        Distance:

Comments:

# 21 Friday 233

Where & When:        Distance:

Comments:

# August

234
_____

**Where & When:**                       **Distance:**

**Comments:**
_____

## Sunday 23

235
_____

**Where & When:**                       **Distance:**

**Comments:**
_____

© -Oxford-/gettyimages

**tip:** New running gear is less likely to chafe if it is laundered first.

**Distance this week:**                       **Weight:**

**Distance carried forward:** _____

# 24 Monday 236
_____
_____
_____

**Where & When:** _____ **Distance:** _____
**Comments:** _____
_____

# 25 Tuesday 237
_____
_____
_____

**Where & When:** _____ **Distance:** _____
**Comments:** _____
_____

# 26 Wednesday 238
_____
_____
_____

**Where & When:** _____ **Distance:** _____
**Comments:** _____
_____

# 27 Thursday 239
_____
_____
_____

**Where & When:** _____ **Distance:** _____
**Comments:** _____
_____

# 28 Friday 240
_____
_____
_____

**Where & When:** _____ **Distance:** _____
**Comments:** _____
_____

# August

**Saturday 29**

---

Where & When:            Distance:

Comments:

242

**Sunday 30**

---

Where & When:            Distance:

Comments:

*"We all have big changes in our lives that are more or less a second chance."*

—Harrison Ford

**tip:** Don't become a slave to daily calorie counts. A runner's body needs more calories on some days than on others.

Notes:

Distance this week:            Weight:

# September

| SUNDAY | MONDAY | TUESDAY | WEDNESDAY | THURSDAY | FRIDAY | SATURDAY |
|--------|--------|---------|-----------|----------|--------|----------|
| | | 1 | 2 | 3 | 4 | 5 |
| 6 | 7 | 8 | 9 | 10 | 11 | 12 |
| Father's Day (Australia, NZ) | Labor Day (USA, Canada) | | | | | |
| 13 | 14 | 15 | 16 | 17 | 18 | 19 |
| | Rosh Hashanah* | | Rosh Hashanah ends | | | |
| 20 | 21 | 22 | 23 | 24 | 25 | 26 |
| | U.N. International Day of Peace | | Yom Kippur* | Eid al-Adha | | |
| 27 | 28 | 29 | 30 | | | |
| | Queen's Birthday (Australia—WA) | | | | | |

*Begins at sundown the previous day

## "The basis of optimism is sheer terror."

—Lord Henry, *The Picture of Dorian Gray* by Oscar Wilde

# HOOEY

We are suckers for science, eager to adopt every new claim or discovery, wide-eyed about innovations in shoe technology, training techniques, or dietary marvels. But don't call us gullible. Runners seek every advantage under foot. Most of the scientific fads we flock toward are harmless, if useless. The challenge is to know when to toss the old junk.

*All runners should stretch before and/or after a workout.* This battle has raged for years. The best evidence is that stretching doesn't make you a better, more agile runner. In fact, stretching before a workout slightly raises the incidence of injury. If you luxuriate in a supple body, save stretching for after your run, and relish it for its own sake, not for its purported benefits. It feels great.

*A warm-down after your run prevents injury and reduces muscle pain.* No runner should doubt the value—consider it a necessity—of a warm-up. Cold muscles should be coaxed into effort. Heart and lungs should be given generous time to dial up their collaboration. But the warm-down at a workout's end is a relatively new orthodoxy. The old science holds that a slow transition to rest prevents muscle soreness and speeds physiological recovery. Unfortunately, it doesn't hold up to scrutiny. A warm-down can prevent pooling of blood in your lower limbs, but a short post-run walk confers the same benefit.

*Well-timed meals enhance performance.* Carbohydrate loading is a proven strategy for building your body's glycogen stores. But a single feast the night before a distance event won't get you there (and may interrupt your run with extra potty trips). Your metabolism and the rate at which your muscles absorb energy are unique. Slowly and deliberately begin adding carbs to your diet at least five days in advance of an event. Likewise, muscles are most greedy for glycogen immediately following a hard race or workout. But shower first. Your performance won't suffer if you can't plunge face first into a bowl of ravioli.

*Cross training will give you a faster finish.* Some evidence suggests that cross training prevents injury. It can improve cardiovascular efficiency, depending on your preferred exercise. Otherwise fitness is tyrannical in the specificity of its demands. If you want to be a faster runner, run. Add speed drills to your workouts for a strong finishing kick.

*Motion-control shoes prevent injury.* When your foot strikes the ground, it pronates—flattens and rolls inward to absorb impact. Because your foot's architecture is unique, how much it pronates is likewise inimitable. It has long been held that over- or under-pronating feet cause injury, so the $6 billion running-shoe industry has invested untold fortunes in designing shoes that correct motion control. Turns out, the problem is pish posh. When buying running shoes, find a comfortable pair, hand the sales clerk your credit card, then run a couple of laps around the block to make your decision. ■

**Distance carried forward:**

## 31 Monday                                                          243

**Where & When:**                                    **Distance:**

**Comments:**

## 1 Tuesday                                                          244

**Where & When:**                                    **Distance:**

**Comments:**

## 2 Wednesday                                                        245

**Where & When:**                                    **Distance:**

**Comments:**

## 3 Thursday                                                         246

**Where & When:**                                    **Distance:**

**Comments:**

## 4 Friday                                                           247

**Where & When:**                                    **Distance:**

**Comments:**

248

## Saturday 5

Where & When: _____ Distance: _____

Comments: _____

249

## Sunday 6

Where & When: _____ Distance: _____

Comments: _____

© Image Source RF/Corey Jenkins/gettyimages

**tip:** Despite the admonitions that running-shoe salespeople may offer, over- or under-pronating feet have no association with injury.

Distance this week: _____ Weight: _____

**Distance carried forward:** _____

# 7 Monday                                          250

_____
_____
_____

Where & When: _____        Distance: _____
Comments: _____
_____

# 8 Tuesday                                         251

_____
_____
_____

Where & When: _____        Distance: _____
Comments: _____
_____

# 9 Wednesday                                       252

_____
_____
_____

Where & When: _____        Distance: _____
Comments: _____
_____

# 10 Thursday                                       253

_____
_____
_____

Where & When: _____        Distance: _____
Comments: _____
_____

# 11 Friday                                         254

_____
_____
_____

Where & When: _____        Distance: _____
Comments: _____
_____

# September

**Saturday 12**

255

Where & When: _____    Distance: _____

Comments: _____

256

**Sunday 13**

Where & When: _____    Distance: _____

Comments: _____

© Zero Creatives/gettyimages

**tip:** Light cardio-exercise is more effective than stretching to prepare your muscles for a hard workout.

Distance this week: _____    Weight: _____

**Distance carried forward:**

# 14 Monday 257

**Where & When:**          **Distance:**

**Comments:**

# 15 Tuesday 258

**Where & When:**          **Distance:**

**Comments:**

# 16 Wednesday 259

**Where & When:**          **Distance:**

**Comments:**

# 17 Thursday 260

**Where & When:**          **Distance:**

**Comments:**

# 18 Friday 261

**Where & When:**          **Distance:**

**Comments:**

# September

**Saturday 19**

_____
_____
_____
_____

**Where & When:** _____ **Distance:** _____

**Comments:** _____

**Sunday 20**

_____
_____
_____
_____

**Where & When:** _____ **Distance:** _____

**Comments:** _____

© Corey Rich/gettyimages

**tip:** Both aerobic exercise and resistance training improve memory.

**Distance this week:** _____ **Weight:** _____

**Distance carried forward:**

## 21 Monday                                                    264

Where & When:                                    Distance:

Comments:

## 22 Tuesday                                                   265

Where & When:                                    Distance:

Comments:

## 23 Wednesday                                                 266

Where & When:                                    Distance:

Comments:

## 24 Thursday                                                  267

Where & When:                                    Distance:

Comments:

## 25 Friday                                                    268

Where & When:                                    Distance:

Comments:

# September

269

Where & When: _____ Distance: _____

Comments: _____

270

**Sunday 27**

Where & When: _____ Distance: _____

Comments: _____

© Chris Giles/gettyimages

**tip:** Don't mistake burnout as a lack of motivation. Dial back the intensity of your workouts.

Distance this week: _____ Weight: _____

**Distance carried forward:** _____

# 28 Monday                                                          271
_____
_____
_____

**Where & When:** _____ **Distance:** _____
**Comments:** _____
_____

# 29 Tuesday                                                         272
_____
_____
_____

**Where & When:** _____ **Distance:** _____
**Comments:** _____
_____

# 30 Wednesday                                                       273
_____
_____
_____

**Where & When:** _____ **Distance:** _____
**Comments:** _____
_____

# 1 Thursday                                                         274
_____
_____
_____

**Where & When:** _____ **Distance:** _____
**Comments:** _____
_____

# 2 Friday                                                           275
_____
_____
_____

**Where & When:** _____ **Distance:** _____
**Comments:** _____
_____

**276** _____ **Saturday 3**

_____
_____
_____

**Where & When:** _____ **Distance:** _____
**Comments:** _____

_____

**277** _____ **Sunday 4**

_____
_____
_____

**Where & When:** _____ **Distance:** _____
**Comments:** _____

_____

*"Desire, both the whispers and the shouts, is the map we have been given to find the only life worth living."*

—John Eldredge, *The Journey of Desire: Searching for the Life We Only Dreamed Of*

**tip:** It's not a myth: Studies show that grocery shopping on an empty stomach does influence food choices.

Notes: _____
_____
_____
_____
_____

**Distance this week:** _____ **Weight:** _____

# October

| SUNDAY | MONDAY | TUESDAY | WEDNESDAY | THURSDAY | FRIDAY | SATURDAY |
|---|---|---|---|---|---|---|
| | | | | 1 | 2 | 3 |
| 4 | 5 <br><br> Labour Day (Australia—ACT, SA, NSW, QLD) | 6 | 7 | 8 | 9 | 10 |
| 11 | 12 <br><br> Columbus Day (USA) <br> Thanksgiving (Canada) | 13 | 14 | 15 | 16 | 17 |
| 18 | 19 | 20 | 21 | 22 | 23 | 24 <br><br> United Nations Day |
| 25 | 26 <br><br> Labour Day (NZ) <br> Bank Holiday (Ireland) | 27 | 28 | 29 | 30 | 31 <br><br> Halloween |

*"Many great actions are committed in small struggles."*
—Victor Hugo

# NUTS

Indulge madness. Don't make a habit of it, but at least once a year set aside a week or so to train crazy. Throw away the agenda, dump the workout routine. Don't seek to prove anything during this exultant delirium. Just surrender to discovery—or rather, rediscovery.

You've done it before. Every training program begins with aches and hopeful possibility, boredom and revelation, great humility, and at least a little silliness. The difference this time around is that you're no longer a beginner. You're far more knowledgeable about your abilities and limitations, more realistic in your expectations. Unfortunately, these virtues may be holding you back.

Timing is crucial when your training program diverts for the nut hut. Obviously, you don't want to go crazy when a race date looms. Nor should you strike out in odd ways when you're just finding a comfortable groove in your workouts. It's when the training effect begins to pay predictable and satisfying dividends—when the peak of fitness is within reach—that you'll find reward in lunacy. This is a paradox, of course. Why mess with what works?

It's because when training turns sweet, you can trust what you learn from it. You're less susceptible to injury. And your body has likely leapt ahead of your ordained goals, eager to show hidden talents. So step on the gas. It's a great time to play around with speed work, which should be a customary part of your workout routine, anyway. Too often we only gradually and methodically add drills to the mix. Ordinarily, there's good sense in this. Still, few competitive distance runners know how long they can sustain a finishing kick. Few noncompetitive runners trust how much speed lies within them. So give yourself over to dedicated speed sets for a couple of weeks. Workout duration will be shorter than the regular drill, and you'll need lots of rest days between them. But they're terribly fun.

The same is true of cross training, in which knowledge gained can be measured in unfamiliar aches and shocking throbs the day after a workout. Running is an elaborate business that draws on supporting muscles from the neck and shoulders (even the face) to the lower back and diaphragm, and dozens of hoists in ankles and feet. Major muscle groups steal our attention. Cross training reintroduces us to neglected corridors of our bodies. It demonstrates the collective effort, the divergent ways a runner grows stronger. It makes you mindful of the instrument at work.

It can also lead you to a new sport or refocused running goals. Don't fear change. Opportunities surge with any form of cross training. But so do illusions and fruitless distraction. The key is to weigh the thrill of novelty against the time a new ambition will steal from running goals. Injury is less of a concern, though it always pays to be wary. An experienced runner understands the limits of ability. It's play, not madness, when you know what you're doing. ∎

**Distance carried forward:**

## 5 Monday
278

Where & When: Distance:

Comments:

## 6 Tuesday
279

Where & When: Distance:

Comments:

## 7 Wednesday
280

Where & When: Distance:

Comments:

## 8 Thursday
281

Where & When: Distance:

Comments:

## 9 Friday
282

Where & When: Distance:

Comments:

# October

283

Where & When:                                                   Distance:

Comments:

284

Where & When:                                                   Distance:

Comments:

© Jordan Siemens/gettyimages

**tip:** Shoes that are too small or too large can cause blisters.

Distance this week:                                             Weight:

**Distance carried forward:** _____

## 12 Monday 285

_____
_____

**Where & When:** _____ **Distance:** _____
**Comments:** _____
_____

## 13 Tuesday 286

_____
_____

**Where & When:** _____ **Distance:** _____
**Comments:** _____
_____

## 14 Wednesday 287

_____
_____

**Where & When:** _____ **Distance:** _____
**Comments:** _____
_____

## 15 Thursday 288

_____
_____

**Where & When:** _____ **Distance:** _____
**Comments:** _____
_____

## 16 Friday 289

_____
_____

**Where & When:** _____ **Distance:** _____
**Comments:** _____
_____

**290**

**Where & When:** | **Distance:**

**Comments:**

**291**

**Where & When:** | **Distance:**

**Comments:**

© Myles Dumas/gettyimages

**tip:** It takes the average person three weeks of sticking with a new activity to make it a habit.

**Distance this week:** | **Weight:**

**Distance carried forward:** _____

# 19 Monday                                                      292

_____
_____
_____

**Where & When:** _____     **Distance:** _____
**Comments:** _____
_____

# 20 Tuesday                                                     293

_____
_____
_____

**Where & When:** _____     **Distance:** _____
**Comments:** _____
_____

# 21 Wednesday                                                   294

_____
_____
_____

**Where & When:** _____     **Distance:** _____
**Comments:** _____
_____

# 22 Thursday                                                    295

_____
_____
_____

**Where & When:** _____     **Distance:** _____
**Comments:** _____
_____

# 23 Friday                                                      296

_____
_____
_____

**Where & When:** _____     **Distance:** _____
**Comments:** _____
_____

# October

297

Where & When: _____ Distance: _____

Comments: _____

298

**Sunday 25**

Where & When: _____ Distance: _____

Comments: _____

© Ryan Lane/gettyimages

**tip:** Even moderate exercise has been shown to lift depression.

Distance this week: _____ Weight: _____

**Distance carried forward:**

# 26 Monday                                          299

Where & When:                          Distance:

Comments:

# 27 Tuesday                                         300

Where & When:                          Distance:

Comments:

# 28 Wednesday                                       301

Where & When:                          Distance:

Comments:

# 29 Thursday                                        302

Where & When:                          Distance:

Comments:

# 30 Friday                                          303

Where & When:                          Distance:

Comments:

**304** _____ **Saturday 31**

_____

_____

_____

**Where & When:** _____ **Distance:** _____

**Comments:** _____

_____

**305** _____ **Sunday 1**

_____

_____

_____

**Where & When:** _____ **Distance:** _____

**Comments:** _____

_____

*"Success is not final, failure is not fatal: It is the courage to continue that counts."*

—Winston Churchill

**tip:** Many gluten-free foods contain twice the carbohydrates and fat than the regular versions, so skip them unless you're especially sensitive to gluten.

Notes: _____

_____

_____

_____

_____

**Distance this week:** _____ **Weight:** _____

# November

| SUNDAY | MONDAY | TUESDAY | WEDNESDAY | THURSDAY | FRIDAY | SATURDAY |
|--------|--------|---------|-----------|----------|--------|----------|
| 1 | 2 | 3 <br><br> Election Day (USA) | 4 | 5 | 6 | 7 |
| 8 | 9 | 10 | 11 <br><br> Veterans' Day (USA) <br> Remembrance Day <br> (Canada, Ireland, UK) | 12 | 13 | 14 |
| 15 | 16 | 17 | 18 | 19 | 20 | 21 |
| 22 | 23 | 24 | 25 | 26 <br><br> Thanksgiving (USA) | 27 | 28 |
| 29 | 30 <br><br> St. Andrew's Day (UK) | | | | | |

*"All you need in this life is ignorance and confidence, and then success is sure."*

—Mark Twain

# MINIMALIST

Let's say you were first badgered into running by a loved one, your doctor, or your own nagging sense that if you plan to survive into dotage, your body needs exercise. You choose running because it intrudes least for the equipment required, time, and expense. It produces solid gains for a minimal investment. Still, you don't really like it. Exactly how little running can get you by?

Even impassioned runners (many who are converts from the I-hate-exercise crowd) are beginning to ask this question. The rise of gyms for the gym-phobic, the 12-weeks-to-a-marathon training programs, the persistent specter of overuse injuries—even the approach of dreary winter weather—urges all runners to ask how much they can scale down without compromising gains or goals. The answer is, quite a lot, so long as you keep honest with yourself.

Core fitness is easiest to maintain with shorter workouts. If you train for health alone, you don't need to run a lot. But you have to build a powerful cardiovascular base before you lighten your weekly commitment. Not only must you strengthen muscles, bones, and supporting hoists and levers, but oxygen and fuel must burn more efficiently. Blood plasma must increase to keep the machine cool. There's mental training, too, the ability to judge the meeting point of stamina and fatigue, to recognize the warning signs of injury, and to stay resolute in the workout at hand. In other words, the training effect should be operating at full speed before you decide to throttle back.

The calendar dictates when a competitive runner can scale down, just as it dictates the training schedule leading up to an event. Unfortunately, the human body doesn't much care about calendars where progress is concerned. Whether you succeed or fail in a race (you and only you must make that call), an abyss opens the day after. It's a perilous time for any training program, whether you're glowing in glory, the efforts now relegated to memory—or recoiling in humiliation and self-doubt. This is when training programs psychologically collapse. Lightening your training schedule allows you to regroup, to direct new ambitions. It gives your body time to heal. Call it treading water, if you like. At least it keeps the endeavor alive.

Of course, most runners pursue multiple goals. Weight management, stress relief, contemplative solitude, or unapologetic vanity all survive a trimmed down workout program, though accommodations in other parts of your life must pitch in to help. How long can you work at a low-burn level of training? Your body will give you the exact answer, but generally, you can scale down mileage or the number of workouts each week by up to 60 percent without noticeable loss of performance. Your age, weight, gender, and weekly mileage all come into account. Short, intense workouts preserve condition better than long, lumbering miles. But they don't build muscle. If you're still plodding through short workouts for more than six weeks, either your interest or abilities have waned. Either way, it's time to reassess. ■

**Distance carried forward:**

## 2 Monday 306

Where & When:                                   Distance:

Comments:

## 3 Tuesday 307

Where & When:                                   Distance:

Comments:

## 4 Wednesday 308

Where & When:                                   Distance:

Comments:

## 5 Thursday 309

Where & When:                                   Distance:

Comments:

## 6 Friday 310

Where & When:                                   Distance:

Comments:

# November

**Saturday 7**

Where & When:                                             Distance:

Comments:

**Sunday 8**

Where & When:                                             Distance:

Comments:

© Jupiterimages/gettyimages

**tip:** If you've been running 9 to 12 miles a week for six months, you're ready to begin serious training for a half marathon. Come up with a plan.

Distance this week:                                      Weight:

**Distance carried forward:** _____

# 9 Monday 313

_____
_____
_____

**Where & When:** _____ **Distance:** _____
**Comments:** _____

# 10 Tuesday 314

_____
_____
_____

**Where & When:** _____ **Distance:** _____
**Comments:** _____

# 11 Wednesday 315

_____
_____
_____

**Where & When:** _____ **Distance:** _____
**Comments:** _____

# 12 Thursday 316

_____
_____
_____

**Where & When:** _____ **Distance:** _____
**Comments:** _____

# 13 Friday 317

_____
_____
_____

**Where & When:** _____ **Distance:** _____
**Comments:** _____

# November

**Saturday 14**

_____

_____

_____

**Where & When:** _____  **Distance:** _____

**Comments:** _____

_____

**Sunday 15**

_____

_____

_____

**Where & When:** _____  **Distance:** _____

**Comments:** _____

_____

© Jordan Siemens/gettyimages

**tip:** Don't overdress for race day. You should feel cool for the first mile or two.

**Distance this week:** _____  **Weight:** _____

**Distance carried forward:**

# 16 Monday 320

Where & When:          Distance:

Comments:

# 17 Tuesday 321

Where & When:          Distance:

Comments:

# 18 Wednesday 322

Where & When:          Distance:

Comments:

# 19 Thursday 323

Where & When:          Distance:

Comments:

# 20 Friday 324

Where & When:          Distance:

Comments:

# November

**325** _____ **Saturday 21**

_____

_____

_____

**Where & When:** _____  **Distance:** _____

**Comments:** _____

_____

**326** _____ **Sunday 22**

_____

_____

_____

**Where & When:** _____  **Distance:** _____

**Comments:** _____

_____

© Blend Images - Erik Isakson/gettyimages

**tip:** When interspersing walking in a race or workout, walk quickly with a short, relaxed stride.

**Distance this week:** _____  **Weight:** _____

**Distance carried forward:**

# 23 Monday
327

**Where & When:**                              **Distance:**

**Comments:**

# 24 Tuesday
328

**Where & When:**                              **Distance:**

**Comments:**

# 25 Wednesday
329

**Where & When:**                              **Distance:**

**Comments:**

# 26 Thursday
330

**Where & When:**                              **Distance:**

**Comments:**

# 27 Friday
331

**Where & When:**                              **Distance:**

**Comments:**

# November

**Saturday 28**

_____
_____
_____

**Where & When:** _____  **Distance:** _____
**Comments:** _____
_____
_____

**Sunday 29**

_____
_____
_____

**Where & When:** _____  **Distance:** _____
**Comments:** _____
_____
_____

_"With regard to excellence, it is not enough to know, but we must try to have and use it."_
—Aristotle

**tip:** Cholesterol-lowering statins, the most widely prescribed class of drugs in the world, can cause muscle aches and fatigue in some patients—especially runners.

Notes: _____
_____
_____
_____
_____

**Distance this week:** _____  **Weight:** _____

# December

| SUNDAY | MONDAY | TUESDAY | WEDNESDAY | THURSDAY | FRIDAY | SATURDAY |
|--------|--------|---------|-----------|----------|--------|----------|
|        |        | 1 | 2 | 3 | 4 | 5 |
| 6 | 7 Hanukkah* | 8 | 9 | 10 Human Rights Day | 11 | 12 |
| 13 | 14 Hanukkah ends | 15 | 16 | 17 | 18 | 19 |
| 20 | 21 | 22 | 23 | 24 Christmas Eve | 25 Christmas Day | 26 Kwanzaa begins (USA) Boxing Day (Canada) St. Stephen's Day (Ireland) |
| 27 | 28 Boxing Day (NZ, UK, Australia—except SA) Proclamation Day (Australia—SA) | 29 | 30 | 31 |  |  |

*Begins at sundown the previous day

"The spirit, the will to win, and the will to excel are the things that endure."

—Cicero

# INFIDELITY

If you always run alone, you can probably say why. To those who ask, you may simply spill a list of banal reasons, knowing that the impulse actually runs deeper. Solo runners rarely brook intrusion. We tend to be protective about our workouts, defiant about their importance, yet secretive about the value they bring to daily living.

We also tend to be arrogant, believing that those who run in packs require external motivation else they won't stick to a training program. At worst, it shows a deficiency of character, a collaborative road to failure. This is not true, and anyone who has competed on a track team or a running club knows that some of the richest, most lasting relationships imaginable—competitive and otherwise—emerge from group training. Just think of the married couples you've met at marathons who first bonded while logging miles together. Does training in pairs lead to love, or the other way around?

Obviously, it doesn't matter, and the calculus for whether you get better results running solo or with others is entirely personal. So you do the math. Meanwhile, promise to invest time in both kinds of workouts, staying keen not to the laundry list of pros and cons each offers, but to where your heart lies. You'll never fully purge the drudgery from training. Faith and familiarity make it bearable. They let you stay focused on larger goals. It's almost as if self-interest surrenders to higher purpose. Just like love.

Best of all, you don't have to be faithful. Many runners make the best of both worlds, mindful of the compromises and irritations of each. The competitive drive of a companion will make you stronger. Shared training time with a friend—even when it's a wordless communion—helps you face a workout when the weather is dodgy or your personal life is troubled. On the other hand, the solemn solo run is the best investment in mental health you can make over time. The laser-like focus it brings to specific goals may seem selfish for the time it steals from others, but the results are abundant and self-affirming. Everyone benefits.

So why not work at both kinds of training? As with paramours, life gets messy when you try to fulfill too many demands. Goals drift, commitment wanes. The thrill of novelty subsides and you're left scattered and unsatisfied. Sure, some solo runners are stronger for weekly dalliances with a partner or group. Some group runners use the occasional solo workout for inventory, to measure improvement. These arrangements are tentative. Most of us need constancy in training in order to measure progress. Most of us are one type of runner or the other.

When setting goals for the coming year, current abilities and ambitions matter less than the type of workouts that bring you personal satisfaction. These are your loyal and abiding partners in success. To find them—and commit—you have to know your own heart. ■

**Distance carried forward:** _____

# 30 Monday 334

_____

**Where & When:** _____ **Distance:** _____

**Comments:** _____

# 1 Tuesday 335

_____

**Where & When:** _____ **Distance:** _____

**Comments:** _____

# 2 Wednesday 336

_____

**Where & When:** _____ **Distance:** _____

**Comments:** _____

# 3 Thursday 337

_____

**Where & When:** _____ **Distance:** _____

**Comments:** _____

# 4 Friday 338

_____

**Where & When:** _____ **Distance:** _____

**Comments:** _____

**339** _____

_____

_____

**Where & When:** _____ **Distance:** _____

**Comments:** _____

_____

**340** _____

**Sunday 6**

_____

_____

**Where & When:** _____ **Distance:** _____

**Comments:** _____

_____

© Chris Christie/gettyimages

**tip:** Road miles don't equal trail miles. When transitioning to trails, measure your workouts with time, not distance.

**Distance this week:** _____ **Weight:** _____

**Distance carried forward:** _____

## 7 Monday 341

_____
_____
_____

**Where & When:** _____  **Distance:** _____

**Comments:**

_____

## 8 Tuesday 342

_____
_____
_____

**Where & When:** _____  **Distance:** _____

**Comments:**

_____

## 9 Wednesday 343

_____
_____
_____

**Where & When:** _____  **Distance:** _____

**Comments:**

_____

## 10 Thursday 344

_____
_____
_____

**Where & When:** _____  **Distance:** _____

**Comments:**

_____

## 11 Friday 345

_____
_____
_____

**Where & When:** _____  **Distance:** _____

**Comments:**

_____

# December

**Saturday 12**

**Where & When:**                        **Distance:**
**Comments:**

**Sunday 13**

**Where & When:**                        **Distance:**
**Comments:**

© Peter Muller/gettyimages

**tip:** If you miss a workout, don't make it up. Just return to your normal training schedule as soon as possible.

**Distance this week:**                        **Weight:**

**Distance carried forward:**

# 14 Monday

Where & When:                                    Distance:

Comments:

# 15 Tuesday

Where & When:                                    Distance:

Comments:

# 16 Wednesday

Where & When:                                    Distance:

Comments:

# 17 Thursday

Where & When:                                    Distance:

Comments:

# 18 Friday

Where & When:                                    Distance:

Comments:

# December

**Saturday 19**

Where & When: _____    Distance: _____

Comments: _____

**Sunday 20**

Where & When: _____    Distance: _____

Comments: _____

© Cultura/Chris Whitehead/gettyimages

**tip:** There is growing evidence that cardio-exercise boosts a flu shot's potency.

**Distance this week:** _____    **Weight:** _____

**Distance carried forward:** _____

# 21 Monday                                                    355
_____
_____

**Where & When:** _____  **Distance:** _____
**Comments:** _____
_____

# 22 Tuesday                                                   356
_____
_____

**Where & When:** _____  **Distance:** _____
**Comments:** _____
_____

# 23 Wednesday                                                 357
_____
_____

**Where & When:** _____  **Distance:** _____
**Comments:** _____
_____

# 24 Thursday                                                  358
_____
_____

**Where & When:** _____  **Distance:** _____
**Comments:** _____
_____

# 25 Friday                                                    359
_____
_____

**Where & When:** _____  **Distance:** _____
**Comments:** _____
_____

# December

## Saturday 26

**Where & When:**           **Distance:**

**Comments:**

## Sunday 27

**Where & When:**           **Distance:**

**Comments:**

© Erik Isakson/gettyimages

**tip:** Another case for strength training: When your upper body tires, your running form deteriorates, and you run less efficiently.

**Distance this week:**           **Weight:**

**Distance carried forward:**

# 28 Monday 362

**Where & When:** **Distance:**

**Comments:**

# 29 Tuesday 363

**Where & When:** **Distance:**

**Comments:**

# 30 Wednesday 364

**Where & When:** **Distance:**

**Comments:**

# 31 Thursday 365

**Where & When:** **Distance:**

**Comments:**

# 1 Friday 366

**Where & When:** **Distance:**

**Comments:**

# Dec/Jan 2016

### Saturday 2

**Where & When:** _____ **Distance:** _____

**Comments:** _____

### Sunday 3

**Where & When:** _____ **Distance:** _____

**Comments:** _____

*"Excellence encourages one about life generally;
it shows the spiritual wealth of the world."*
—George Eliot

**tip:** It's true that reducing salt consumption will lower your blood pressure. But claims that it will reduce hypertension, prevent heart disease, or lengthen life have no evidence.

Notes: _____

**Distance this week:** _____ **Weight:** _____

# Twelve Months of Running

| | | | | | | | | | | | | |
|---|---|---|---|---|---|---|---|---|---|---|---|---|
| | | | | | | | | | | | | |
| | | | | | | | | | | | | |
| | | | | | | | | | | | | |
| | | | | | | | | | | | | |
| | | | | | | | | | | | | |
| | | | | | | | | | | | | |
| | | | | | | | | | | | | |
| Jan. 5 | Jan. 12 | Jan. 19 | Jan. 26 | Feb. 2 | Feb. 9 | Feb. 16 | Feb. 23 | March 2 | March 9 | March 16 | March 23 | March 30 |

To create a cumulative bar graph of weekly mileage,
apply an appropriate scale at the left-hand margin.
Then fill in the bar for each week of running.

| | Apr. 6 | Apr. 13 | Apr. 20 | Apr. 27 | May 4 | May 11 | May 18 | May 25 | June 1 | June 8 | June 15 | June 22 | June 29 |
|---|---|---|---|---|---|---|---|---|---|---|---|---|---|
| | | | | | | | | | | | | | |

To create a cumulative bar graph of weekly mileage,
apply an appropriate scale at the left-hand margin.
Then fill in the bar for each week of running.

| | July 6 | July 13 | July 20 | July 27 | Aug. 3 | Aug. 10 | Aug. 17 | Aug. 24 | Aug. 31 | Sept. 7 | Sept. 14 | Sept. 21 | Sept. 28 |
|---|---|---|---|---|---|---|---|---|---|---|---|---|---|

To create a cumulative bar graph of weekly mileage,
apply an appropriate scale at the left-hand margin.
Then fill in the bar for each week of running.

| Oct. 5 | Oct. 12 | Oct. 19 | Oct. 26 | Nov. 2 | Nov. 9 | Nov. 16 | Nov. 23 | Nov. 30 | Dec. 7 | Dec. 14 | Dec. 21 | Dec. 28 |
|--------|---------|---------|---------|--------|--------|---------|---------|---------|--------|---------|---------|---------|

# A Record of Races

| Date | Place | Distance | Time | Pace | Comments & Excuses |
|------|-------|----------|------|------|--------------------|
|      |       |          |      |      |                    |
|      |       |          |      |      |                    |
|      |       |          |      |      |                    |
|      |       |          |      |      |                    |
|      |       |          |      |      |                    |
|      |       |          |      |      |                    |
|      |       |          |      |      |                    |
|      |       |          |      |      |                    |
|      |       |          |      |      |                    |
|      |       |          |      |      |                    |
|      |       |          |      |      |                    |
|      |       |          |      |      |                    |
|      |       |          |      |      |                    |
|      |       |          |      |      |                    |
|      |       |          |      |      |                    |
|      |       |          |      |      |                    |
|      |       |          |      |      |                    |
|      |       |          |      |      |                    |
|      |       |          |      |      |                    |
|      |       |          |      |      |                    |
|      |       |          |      |      |                    |
|      |       |          |      |      |                    |
|      |       |          |      |      |                    |
|      |       |          |      |      |                    |
|      |       |          |      |      |                    |
|      |       |          |      |      |                    |
|      |       |          |      |      |                    |
|      |       |          |      |      |                    |
|      |       |          |      |      |                    |
|      |       |          |      |      |                    |
|      |       |          |      |      |                    |
|      |       |          |      |      |                    |
|      |       |          |      |      |                    |
|      |       |          |      |      |                    |
|      |       |          |      |      |                    |
|      |       |          |      |      |                    |
|      |       |          |      |      |                    |
|      |       |          |      |      |                    |

# A Record of Races

| Date | Place | Distance | Time | Pace | Comments & Excuses |
|------|-------|----------|------|------|--------------------|
|      |       |          |      |      |                    |
|      |       |          |      |      |                    |
|      |       |          |      |      |                    |
|      |       |          |      |      |                    |
|      |       |          |      |      |                    |
|      |       |          |      |      |                    |
|      |       |          |      |      |                    |
|      |       |          |      |      |                    |
|      |       |          |      |      |                    |
|      |       |          |      |      |                    |
|      |       |          |      |      |                    |
|      |       |          |      |      |                    |
|      |       |          |      |      |                    |
|      |       |          |      |      |                    |
|      |       |          |      |      |                    |
|      |       |          |      |      |                    |
|      |       |          |      |      |                    |
|      |       |          |      |      |                    |
|      |       |          |      |      |                    |
|      |       |          |      |      |                    |
|      |       |          |      |      |                    |
|      |       |          |      |      |                    |
|      |       |          |      |      |                    |
|      |       |          |      |      |                    |
|      |       |          |      |      |                    |
|      |       |          |      |      |                    |
|      |       |          |      |      |                    |
|      |       |          |      |      |                    |
|      |       |          |      |      |                    |
|      |       |          |      |      |                    |
|      |       |          |      |      |                    |
|      |       |          |      |      |                    |
|      |       |          |      |      |                    |
|      |       |          |      |      |                    |
|      |       |          |      |      |                    |
|      |       |          |      |      |                    |
|      |       |          |      |      |                    |
|      |       |          |      |      |                    |

# RACING

Pace is crucial. And you won't magically find it on race day. If you've resisted using a stopwatch or a heart monitor in your workouts, training for a 10K race is the perfect opportunity to abandon those prejudices.

*Divide the race into three equal segments and start slower than you want. Don't reach your race pace until the second segment. Push on the third. But your times between these three segments shouldn't vary by more than 10 percent.*

## 10K

Warm up? Yes, even a slow half-mile run before the race is likely to improve your performance, not fatigue you. Remember that a 10K event is too short to grant you a sufficient warm-up during the race.

## Half Marathon

*If you're running a half-marathon as preparation for a marathon, cut your weekly long run to no more than 12 miles and raise the pace.*

Every week should include three types of workouts: speed drills, tempo runs, and your long run. Speed drills make you faster. Tempo runs raise your lactate threshold, which will help you maintain a racing pace in the second half of the event. And your weekly long run increases endurance. Toss in some cross training when time allows.

Don't be shaken by early mistakes. If you go out too fast, for example, simply dial back as soon as you recognize your error. It's a long race and there's plenty of time to recover from just about any kind of blunder.

# Marathon

*No one masters the marathon. Anything can happen on its long tortuous course, which is why it is such a seductive and exciting event. It's in your interest to arrive at the starting line with this humility.*

Seek support. Train with a partner or a running group. Get your loved ones to cheer you on at the race. Raise money for a cause. The road to the marathon can be long and lonely. Let others help you get there.

**Believe it or not, it's better to undertrain than to overtrain. What you haven't developed by race day can sometimes be overcome with adrenalin and desire. For an overtrained runner, the race is over before it starts.**

**Get used to crowding. In open water where visibility is often poor, contact with other swimmers is inevitable. On bicycles it can be dangerous. Patience pays. Fighting through a pack of competitors wastes energy and can throw your race into jeopardy. Relax. Your opportunity to pass will come.**

# Triathlon

*Rehearse transitions. Without specific training, it takes bicycling legs longer to reach their running stride than many athletes realize. Pulling dry socks onto wet feet can be an ordeal. Fussing with uncooperative equipment squanders time.*

Your weakest event deserves the greatest amount of training effort. Sorry, it's true. Most triathletes use their best event to make up time. The better strategy is not to lose time in your weak event.

## JANUARY 2016

_____
_____
_____
_____
_____

## FEBRUARY 2016

_____
_____
_____
_____
_____

## MARCH 2016

_____
_____
_____
_____
_____

## APRIL 2016

_____
_____
_____
_____
_____

## MAY 2016

_____
_____
_____
_____
_____

## JUNE 2016

_____
_____
_____
_____
_____

## JULY 2016

_____
_____
_____
_____
_____

## AUGUST 2016

_____
_____
_____
_____
_____

## SEPTEMBER 2016

_____
_____
_____
_____
_____

## OCTOBER 2016

_____
_____
_____
_____
_____

## NOVEMBER 2016

_____
_____
_____
_____
_____

## DECEMBER 2016

_____
_____
_____
_____
_____